NORFOLK

A GENEALOGICAL BIBLIOGRAPHY

— BY —
STUART A. RAYMOND

GW00566730

FEDERATION OF FAMILY HISTORY SOCIETIES

Published by the
Federation of Family History Societies,
c/o The Benson Room, Birmingham & Midland Institute,
Margaret Street, Birmingham, B3 3BS, U.K.

Copies also available from:
S.A. & M.J. Raymond, 6 Russet Avenue, Exeter, Devon, EX1 3QB, U.K.

Text processed and printed by
Oxuniprint, Oxford University Press

Cataloguing in publication data:

RAYMOND, Stuart A., 1945- .
Norfolk: a genealogical bibliography. British genealogical bibliographies.
Birmingham, England: Federation of Family History Societies, 1993.

DDC: 016.9291094261

ISBN: 1 872094 59 7

ISSN: 1033-2065

CONTENTS

INTRODUCTION

This bibliography is intended primarily for genealogists. It is hoped, however, that it will also prove useful to local historians, librarians, research students, and anyone else interested in the history of Norfolk and its families. It is designed to be used in conjunction with my *English genealogy: an introductory bibliography* which lists general work relating to the whole of England, and with the other volumes in the *British genealogical bibliographies* series.

Many genealogists fail to appreciate just how much material likely to be of interest to them has been published. Not infrequently, they head for the archives before checking out printed sources first. When faced by the vast array of printed tomes to be found in places such as the Norfolk Record Office, they do not know where to begin. This bibliography, in conjunction with others in the series, is intended to point you in the right direction. It is as complete as I have been able to make it. Be warned, however—I make no pretensions to comprehensiveness. Neither do I claim total accuracy. Both these aims are beyond the abilities of any bibliographer. Most items I have seen, but some I have not. Some things I have deliberately excluded; others I have undoubtedly missed. If you come across anything I have missed, please let me know, so that it may be included in a second edition if required. There are innumerable brief notes in journals such as *E.A.M.* and *N.Anc.*, these are not listed here unless they include original sources or are otherwise relatively substantial. Replies to such notes, where given, are listed in the form 'see also', with no author's name given. Local and church histories have also been excluded, except in a few cases. Such histories are frequently invaluable for genealogical purposes, but a full listing would require another volume. This is a bibliography of published works; therefore, the many unpublished family histories and transcripts of original sources to be found in places such as Norwich Public Library are not included.

Most works listed here are readily available in the libraries listed below—although no library holds everything. Even if you are overseas, you should be able to find copies of the more important reference works in larger research libraries. However, some items may prove difficult to locate—particularly articles in local periodicals. Never fear! Librarians believe in the doctrine of the universal availability of publications, and most public libraries are able to tap into the international inter-library loans system. Your local library should be able to borrow most of the items listed here, even if it has to go overseas to obtain them.

A word of warning. When using any of the works listed here, you must remember that the publication of a work is no guarantee of its accuracy. Many editions of original source materials are highly competent—but others are woeful. You may well need to check the information found in printed books against the original documents in the archives.

The work of compiling this bibliography was undertaken primarily in Exeter, although I also spent time in Oxford, London, Bristol, Taunton, Ipswich and Bury St.Edmunds. The most important libraries used included Exeter Public Library, Exeter University Library, the British Library, the Bodleian Library, Bristol University Library, Suffolk Record Office and Somerset Archaeological and Natural History Society. I am grateful to the librarians of all these institutions for their help. My manuscript was typed by Terry Humphries, and read by Charles Farrow. Bob Boyd saw it through the press, and Jeremy Gibson provided much needed support. I have also had assistance from the Norfolk and Norwich Genealogical Society, Norfolk Record Office, and Norfolk County Library. My grateful thanks to all these people, and also to the officers of the Federation of Family History Societies, whose support is vital to the success of this series.

Stuart A. Raymond

ABBREVIATIONS

E.A.M.	*East Anglian Miscellany*
F.N.Q.	*Fenland Notes and Queries*
M.G.H.	*Miscellanea Genealogica et Heraldica*
N.A.	*Norfolk Archaeology*
N.Anc.	*Norfolk Ancestor*
N.A.M.	*Norfolk Antiquarian Miscellany*
N.N.G.S.	Norfolk and Norwich Genealogical Society
N.N.N.Q.	*Norfolk and Norwich Notes and Queries*
N.N.R.	*Norfolk Nonconformist Registers*
N.P.R.M.	*Norfolk Parish Registers: Marriages*
N.R.S.	Norfolk Record Society
P.P.R.S.	*Phillimore's Parish Register Series*
P.R.N.	Parish Registers of Norfolk, Monograph Series

LIBRARIES AND RECORD OFFICES

Norfolk County Library
Central Library
Bethel Street
NORWICH
NR2 1NJ

Norfolk Record Office
Central Library
Bethel Street
NORWICH
NR2 1NY

The Library
University of East Anglia
NORWICH
NR4 7TJ

Norfolk and Norwich Genealogical Society
Kirby House
38 St.Giles Street
NORWICH
NR2 1LL
(Members only)

BIBLIOGRAPHIC PRESENTATION

Authors' names are in SMALL CAPITALS. Book and journal titles are in *italics*. Articles appearing in journals, and material such as parish register transcripts, forming only part of books, are in inverted commas and textface type. Volume numbers are in **bold** and the individual number of the journal may be shown in parentheses. These are normally followed by the place of publication (except where this is London, which is omitted), the name of the publisher and the date of publication. In the case of articles, further figures indicate page numbers.

1. THE HISTORY OF NORFOLK

How did your ancestors live, work, eat and sleep? What was the world they lived in like? If you want to know the answers to questions like these, and to understand the world of monumental inscriptions, parish registers and probate records, you need to study local history. A good general survey of Norfolk history is provided by:

MARTINS, SUSANNA WADE. *A history of Norfolk.* Darwen county history series. Chichester: Phillimore, 1984.

Older histories include:

MASON, ROBERT HINDRY. *The history of Norfolk, compiled chiefly from original records and other authorities preserved in public and private collections.* Wertheimer Lea & Co., 1884. Incomplete; only that part dealing with the medieval period was printed.

RYE, WALTER. *A history of Norfolk.* Elliot Stock, 1885.

BRIERS, FRANK, ed. *Norwich and its region.* Norwich: British Association for the Advancement of Science, 1961.

There are a number of essay collections:

KETTON-CREMER, R.W. *Norfolk portraits.* Faber & Faber, 1944. Biographies of eminent persons.

KETTON-CREMER, R.W. *Norfolk assembly.* Faber & Faber, 1957.

KETTON-CREMER, R.W. *Forty Norfolk essays.* Norwich: Jarrold & Sons, 1961.

KETTON-CREMER, ROBERT WYNDHAM. *A Norfolk gallery.* Faber, 1948. Mainly biographies of notables.

RYE, WALTER. *Some historical essays chiefly relating to Norfolk.* Norwich: [ ], 1925-8.

For the genealogist, the most useful histories are those which provide accounts of individual parishes, and include extracts from monumental inscriptions, parish registers, wills, and other sources. A number of such parochial surveys exist for Norfolk; the oldest is:

HOOD, CHRISTOBEL M., ed. *The chorography of Norfolk: an historicall and chorographicall description of Norffolck.* Norwich: Jarrold & Sons, 1938. Written c.1600, and attributed to John Norden. Includes many descents of manors.

BLOMEFIELD, FRANCIS. *An essay towards a topographical history of the county of Norfolk ...* 2nd ed. 11 vols. Continued from vol.6 by Charles Parkin. William Miller, 1805-10. Gives lists of rectors, descents of manors, many pedigrees, monumental inscriptions, etc. The author was not always as careful a genealogist as he might have been, but this is a monumental work, and has provided the basis from which later historians have worked. Indexes are provided in:

'An index to the names of the manors mentioned in Blomefield's *Norfolk* (8vo. ed.)', *N.A.M.* 2, 1883, 285-304.

CHADWICK, JOHN NURSE. *Index nominum, being an index of christian and surnames (with arms) mentioned in Blomefield's* History of Norfolk. Kings Lynn: the author, 1862.

Blomefield's work is supplemented by:

INGLEBY, CLEMENT, ed. *A supplement to Blomefield's* Norfolk, *being a series of articles on the antiquities of the county contributed by many distinguished antiquarians ...* The Editor, 1929.

TURNER, DAWSON. *Catalogue of engravings, etchings, and original drawings and deeds, collected towards the illustration of the topography of Norfolk, and inserted in a copy of Blomefield's History of that county in the library of Dawson Turner at Yarmouth.* [ ]: [ ], 1841. Lists many monumental inscriptions; also portraits, etc.

A further parochial survey is provided by:

BRYANT, T.H. *Norfolk churches.* 17 vols. Norwich: Norwich Mercury, 1890-1906. Initially published in the *Norwich Mercury.* The subject matter is much wider than the title suggests. This is a parochial survey, with a volume for each hundred; it includes lists of clergy, manorial notes, monumental inscriptions, etc., etc., and is continued in a different format by:

BRYANT, T. HUGH. *The churches of Norfolk: Hundred of Diss.* Norwich: Norwich Mercury, 1915. Includes lists of clergy, monumental inscriptions, manorial notes, etc., etc.

BRYANT, T. HUGH. *The churches of Norfolk: Hundred of Brothercross.* Norwich: Norwich Mercury, 1914.

BRYANT, T. HUGH. *The churches of Norfolk: Hundred of Shropham.* Norwich: Norwich Mercury, 1913.

A number of similar parochial surveys covering small areas within the county are also available:

RYE, WALTER. *Cromer, past and present, or, an attempt to describe the parishes of Shipden and Cromer, and to narrate their history.* Norwich: Jarrold and Sons, 1889. Includes monumental inscriptions, subsidy rolls, list of wills, etc.

CARTHEW, G.A. *A history, topographical, archaeological, genealogical, and biographical, of the parishes of West and East Bradenham, with those of Necton and Holme Hale, in the county of Norfolk, from public records, court rolls, wills, parish registers and private sources.* ed. Augustus Jessopp. Norwich: A.H. Goose & Co., 1883. Includes many pedigrees and extracts from original records.

CARTHEW, G.A. *The Hundred of Launditch and Deanery of Brisley, in the county of Norfolk: evidences and topographical notes from public records, heralds' visitations, wills, court rolls, old charters, parish registers, town books and other private sources.* 3 vols. Norwich: Miller and Leavins, 1877-9. Marred by many errors of transcription. Vol.3 includes corrections to Blomefield. Includes many pedigrees.

RYE, WALTER. *Some rough materials for a history of the Hundred of North Erpingham in the County of Norfolk.* 3 vols. Norwich: Agas H. Goose, 1885-9. Includes many original sources, e.g. tax rolls, poll books, fines, monumental inscriptions, etc.

The authoritative *Victoria County History* is not complete for Norfolk; only two volumes have been published:

The Victoria history of the County of Norfolk. 2 vols. to date. Westminster: Archibald Constable, 1901-6. v.2. includes Domesday Book, ecclesiastical history, political history, etc.

There are innumerable general works on the history of the county. The list which follows is arranged in rough chronological order. This is very much a personal selection, and emphasises recent works which use genealogical sources for more general historical inquiry. There are numerous other county and local studies of Norfolk, many of which have genealogical value. Parish histories in particular often contain much genealogical information. However, whilst a few are listed in this book, a full listing is not possible here. For help in identifying them, consult the volumes listed in section 2 below.

DYMOND, DAVID. *The Norfolk landscape.* The making of the English landscape series. Hodder & Stoughton, 1985.

DARBY, H.C. *The medieval Fenland.* Cambridge: C.U.P., 1940.

DARBY, H.C. *The changing Fenland.* Cambridge: C.U.P., 1983.

DARBY, H.C. *The draining of the Fens.* 2nd ed. Cambridge: C.U.P., 1956.

BATES, MARTIN. *East Anglia: Norfolk, Suffolk, Essex, Cambridgeshire.* Regional military histories. Reading: Osprey, 1974.

DOUGLAS, DAVID C. *The social structure of medieval East Anglia.* Oxford studies in social and legal history 9. Oxford: Clarendon Press, 1927. Suffolk and Norfolk, 12-13th c.

SAUL, ANTHONY. 'English towns in the late middle ages: the case of Great Yarmouth', *Journal of Medieval History* 8, 1982, 75-88.

WILLIAMSON, JANET. 'Norfolk: the thirteenth century', in HARVEY, P.D.A., ed. *The peasant land market in medieval England.* Oxford: Clarendon Press, 1984, 30-105.

CLARK, ELAINE. 'The decision to marry in thirteenth and early fourteenth-century Norfolk', *Medieval Studies* 49, 1987, 496-516. Based on court rolls of Salle, Horsham St.Faith, and other manors.

RUTLEDGE, ELIZABETH. 'Immigration and population growth in early fourteenth-century Norwich: evidence from the tithing roll', *Urban History Yearbook* 1988, 15-30.

GLASSCOCK, R.E. 'The distribution of wealth in East Anglia in the early 14th century', *Transactions of the Institute of British Geographers* 32, 1963, 113-23. Based on the subsidy.

BEAUROY, J. 'Family patterns and relations of Bishops' Lynn will-makers in the fourteenth century', in BONFIELD, LLOYD, SMITH, RICHARD M., & WRIGHTSON, KEITH, eds. *The world we have gained: histories of population and social structure: essays presented to Peter Laslett on his seventieth birthday.* Oxford: Blackwell, 1986, 23-42. Now Kings Lynn.

CAMPBELL, BRUCE S. 'Population pressure, inheritance and the land market in a fourteenth-century peasant community', in SMITH, RICHARD M., ed. *Land, kinship, and life-cycle.* Cambridge: C.U.P., 1984, 87-134. Based on the manorial court rolls of Coltishall.

CORNFORD, BARBARA, ed. *Studies towards a history of the rising of 1381 in Norfolk.* Norwich: Norfolk Research Committee, 1984. Based partially on manorial records.

JORDAN, W.K. *The Charities of rural England, 1480-1660: the aspirations and achievements of the rural society.* George Allen & Unwin, 1961. Based on wills of Buckinghamshire, Norfolk and Yorkshire.

POUND, JOHN. *Tudor and Stuart Norwich.* Chichester: Phillimore, 1988.

AMUSSEN, SUSAN DWYER. *An ordered society: gender and class in early modern England.* Oxford: Basil Blackwell, 1988. Concerns mainly Cawston, Winfarthing, Shelfanger, Stow Bardolph and Wimbotsham.

EVANS, NESTA. *The East Anglian linen industry: rural industry and local economy, 1500-1850.* Pasold studies in textile history **5**. Aldershot: Gower, 1985. Largely based on probate and poor law records.

HOULBROOKE, R.A. *Church courts and the people during the English Reformation, 1520-1570.* Oxford: Oxford University Press, 1979. Based on the records of the Dioceses of Norwich and Winchester.

POUND, J.F. 'The social and trade structure of Norwich, 1525-1575', *Past and present* **34**, 1966, 49-69.

RUSSELL, F.W. *Ketts Rebellion in Norfolk ...* Longman, Brown, Green, Longmans & Roberts, 1859. Includes a pedigree of Kett, 14-19th c., and many original documents.

BINDOFF, S.T. *Ket's rebellion, 1549.* General series **12**. Historical Association, 1949.

CORNWALL, J. *Revolt of the peasantry, 1549.* Routledge & Kegan Paul, 1977. Study of the risings in Norfolk and the South West.

LAND, STEPHEN K. *Ketts rebellion: the Norfolk rising of 1549.* Ipswich: Boydell Press, 1977. Includes chapter on the Kett family.

SLACK, PAUL, ed. *Rebellion, popular protest and the social order in early modern England.* Cambridge: C.U.P., 1984. Includes a debate on Kett's rebellion.

SWALES, T.H. 'The redistribution of monastic lands in Norfolk at the Dissolution', *N.A.* **34**, 1969, 14-44.

CRESSY, D. 'Levels of illiteracy in England, 1530-1730', *Historical journal* **20**, 1977, 1-23. Based on the depositions of the Consistory Court of the Diocese of Norwich.

HOULBROOKE, RALPH. 'The making of marriage in mid-Tudor England: evidence from the records of matrimonial contract litigation', *Journal of family history* **10**(4), 1985, 339-52.

SMITH, A. HASSELL *County and court: government and politics in Norfolk, 1558-1603.* Oxford: Clarendon Press, 1974. Important.

SMITH, A. HASSELL. 'Justices at work in Elizabethan Norfolk', *N.A.* **34**, 1969, 93-110.

POUND, J.F. 'An Elizabethan census of the poor: the treatment of vagrancy in Norwich, 1570-1580', *University of Birmingham historical journal* **8**(2), 1962, 135-61. General discussion based on the Norwich census of the poor (see below, section 17).

PELLING, MARGARET. 'Illness among the poor in an early modern English town: the Norwich census of 1570', *Continuity and change* **3**, 1988, 273-90.

OVERTON, MARK. 'Estimating crop yields from probate inventories: an example from East Anglia', *Journal of economic history* **39**, 1979, 363-78. Norfolk and Suffolk.

WALES, TIM. 'Poverty, poor relief, and the life-cycle: some evidence from seventeenth-century Norfolk', in SMITH, RICHARD M., ed. *Land, kinship and life-cycle.* Cambridge: C.U.P., 1984, 351-404. Based on overseers accounts.

EVANS, JOHN T. *Seventeenth-Century Norwich: politics, religion and government, 1620-1690.* Oxford: Clarendon Press, 1979.

KETTON-CREMER, R.W. *Norfolk in the Civil War: a portrait of a society in conflict.* Faber, 1969.

KINGSTON, ALFRED. *East Anglia and the Great Civil War: the rising of Cromwell's Ironsides in the associated counties of Cambridge, Huntingdon, Lincoln, Norfolk, Suffolk, Essex and Hertford.* Elliot Stock, 1902. Includes lists of the Committeemen.

HOLMES, CLIVE. *The Eastern Association in the English Civil War.* Cambridge: C.U.P., 1974.

HOLDERNESS, B.A. 'Credit in English rural society before the nineteenth century, with special reference to the period 1650-1720', *Agricultural History Review* **24**, 1976, 97-109. Based partly on Norfolk probate inventories.

PRIESTLEY, URSULA, & FENNER, ALAYNE. *Shops and shopkeepers in Norwich, 1660-1730.* Norwich: University of East Anglia Centre of East Anglian Studies, 1985. Based on tradesmens' probate inventories.

BANKS, SARAH. 'Parish landownership and the land tax assessments in West Norfolk: a comparison with the tithe surveys', in TURNER, MICHAEL, & MILLS, DENNIS., eds. *Land and property: the English land tax 1692-1832.* Gloucester: Alan Sutton, 1986, 39-52.

MARTINS, SUSANNA WADE. *A great estate at work: the Holkham estate and its inhabitants in the nineteenth century.* Cambridge: C.U.P., 1980. Includes pedigree of Coke, 18-20th c.

EDWARDS, J.K. 'Norwich bills of mortality, 1707-1830', *Yorkshire bulletin economic and social research* **21**, 1969, 94-113.

RICHES, NAOMI. *The agricultural revolution in Norfolk.* Chapel Hill: University of North Carolina Press, 1937.

CARTER, MICHAEL J. *Peasants and poachers: a study in rural disorder in Norfolk.* Woodbridge: Boydell Press, 1980. 19th c.

DIGBY, ANNE. *Pauper palaces.* Routledge, 1978. Study of the 19th c. poor law in Norfolk.

SPRINGALL, L. MARION. *Labouring life in Norfolk villages, 1834-1914.* George Allen & Unwin, 1936.

HOWKINS, ALUN. *Poor labouring men: rural radicalism in Norfolk, 1872-1923.* History Workshop series. Routledge & Kegan Paul, 1985.

HOWKINS, ALUN. 'Structural conflict and the farmworker: Norfolk, 1900-1920', *Journal of Peasant Studies* **4**, 1977, 217-29.

2. BIBLIOGRAPHY AND ARCHIVES

The literature of Norfolk history has provided work for many bibliographers. The standard work is now:

DARROCH, ELIZABETH, & TAYLOR, BARRY. *A bibliography of Norfolk history.* [Norwich]: University of East Anglia, 1975.

This is updated by:

TAYLOR, BARRY. *A bibliography of Norfolk history, II: 1974-1988.* Norwich: Centre of East Anglian Studies, University of East Anglia, 1991.

An essential guide to both original and printed sources relating to particular parishes is provided by:

PALGRAVE-MOORE, PATRICK. *Norfolk genealogy: a topographical index of printed and manuscript material in both public and private hands relating to Norfolk genealogy.* 2 vols. Norfolk genealogy, **1** & **2**, 1969-70.

For listings of more recent works, see:

East Anglian bibliography: a checklist of publications not in the British National Bibliography Library Association (Eastern Branch), 1960-

If you live in East Anglia, and want to consult some of the works listed here, see:

HUMPHREY, ELIZABETH. *Periodicals and sets relating to British history in Norfolk and Suffolk libraries: a finding list.* University of East Anglia Centre of East Anglian Studies, [1970]. Includes listings of poll books, parish magazines, local society publications, directories, etc., as well as national publications.

A useful guide to local libraries is provided by:

HUMPHREY, ELIZABETH. *History collections in Norfolk and Suffolk libraries: a handbook.* Norwich: University of East Anglia Library, [1970].

Theses in general are almost totally ignored by genealogists. Yet some could provide useful clues. For a list, see:

BAKER, GILLIAN. *East Anglian history: theses completed.* Norwich: University of East Anglia Centre of East Anglian Studies, 1972.

HENNEY, JANICE. *East Anglian studies: theses completed.* Norwich: Centre of East Anglian Studies, 1982.

There are a variety of older bibliographical works still worth consultation. Walter Rye was responsible for a number of these:

RYE, WALTER. *A handbook to the materials available to students of local history and genealogy, arranged in order of date.* Rye's Norfolk handbooks, N.S. **1**. Norwich: H.W. Hunt, 1924. A brief but useful listing of manuscripts and books.

RYE, WALTER. *An index to Norfolk topography.* Index Society publications **10**. Longmans Green & Co., 1881. Indexes by place a great mass of manuscript and printed materials from various collections. Supplemented by:

RYE, WALTER. *An appendix to Rye's Index to Norfolk topography.* Rye's Norfolk handlists, 2nd series **1**. Norwich: Roberts & Co., 1916. See also his *Index to Norfolk pedigrees*, listed in section 5.

RYE, WALTER. *An index rerum to Norfolk antiquities.* Norwich: Agas H. Goose, 1899. Subject index to Norfolk books and journals.

See also:

WOODWARD, SAMUEL. *The Norfolk topographer's manual, being a catalogue of the books and engravings hitherto published in relation to the county.* rev. W.C. Ewing. Nichols and Son, 1842. Includes, as appendices, a list of *Original drawings, engravings, etchings and deeds &c &c. inserted in a copy of Blomefield's History of Norfolk in the library of Dawson Turner, esq., at Yarmouth* (which includes many monumental inscriptions), also *Short notices of such of the contents of the Harleian, Cottonian, Lansdowne and other manuscripts in the British Museum as refer to Norfolk,* and *List of the chartularies as far as they are known to exist of Norfolk monasteries.*

[DE CASTRE, W.] *A handlist of some manuscript indexes to Norfolk and Suffolk works.* [ ]: [ ], [1920]. Lists various indices to be found in local public libraries.

The major collection of books on Norfolk is at Norwich Public Library. Its early 20th c. catalogue was published in two places:

RYE, WALTER. 'A short calendar of the topographical and genealogical books and mss. in the Free Library at Norwich', *N.A.M.* 2nd series **2**, 1907, 10-54.

RYE, WALTER. *A catalogue of the topographical and antiquarian portions of the Free Library at Norwich.* Norwich: Gibbs & Waller, 1908.

The contents of a useful modern collection more specifically intended for the genealogist are briefly described in:

'The Society library', *N.Anc.* **2**(10), 1982, 130-33. The library of the Norfolk & Norwich Genealogical Society.

For a fuller listing, see:

NORFOLK AND NORWICH GENEALOGICAL SOCIETY. *List of accessions.* [Norwich]: N.N.G.S., 1991. Includes both printed and manuscript material, including many transcripts of parish records, monumental inscriptions, census returns, and unpublished histories, pedigrees and notes on particular families. Additions to the library are regularly noted in *N.Anc.*

The history of Norwich has been the subject of two bibliographies—both, unfortunately, now very old:

STEPHEN, GEORGE ARTHUR. *Guide to the study of Norwich: a select bibliography of the principal books, pamphlets and articles on Norwich in the Norwich Public Library.* 2nd ed. Norwich: Public Library Committee, 1919.

RYE, WALTER. 'An attempt at a general index to the topography of the city of Norwich', *N.A.M.* **1**, 1877, 437-60. Index of various printed works.

Archives

The major collection of archival sources is at the Norfolk Record Office. For its genealogical holdings, see:

NORFOLK RECORD OFFICE. *Guide to genealogical sources.* Norwich: Norfolk Record Office, 1988.

See also:

GRACE, MARY. 'The document and manuscript collection of the Norfolk and Norwich Record Office', *Genealogists magazine* **15**, 1965-8, 200-7. General discussion of genealogical sources, now somewhat outdated.

KENNEDY, JEAN. 'Local archives of Great Britain, XXX: the Norfolk and Norwich Record Office', *Archives* **8**(38), 1967, 63-9.

Various authors, especially Rye, have attempted to list relevant materials in a variety of record repositories:

RYE, WALTER. 'The unpublished material for a history of the county of Norfolk', *Archaeological journal* **47**, 1890, 164-9.

RYE, WALTER. 'Mss. in the Public Record Office relating to Norfolk', *N.A.* **7**, 1872, 137-52.

RYE, WALTER. 'Manuscripts relating to Norfolk in the Harleian and Cottonian libraries', *East Anglian* **2**, 1866, 330-1 & 336-8.

RYE, WALTER. 'Norfolk genealogy and heraldry', *N.A.M.* **3**, 1887, 168-76. List of important manuscripts in various repositories.

Bibliography and Archives *continued*

EDWARDS, LAWSON. *Norfolk sources at the Society of Genealogists Library*. Norwich: N.N.G.S., 1989. Brief pamphlet.

The collections of a number of Norfolk antiquarians and historians have been considered in print; the relevant works are listed here, together with bibliographies of the works of two prolific Norfolk authors.

Blomefield

COZENS-HARDY, BASIL. 'Calendar of such of the Frere mss. as relate to the Hundred of Holt', *N.R.S.* **1**, 1931, 5-40. Materials collected by Blomefield.

LINNELL, C.L.S. 'Some notes on the Blomefield ms. in the Bodleian Library', *N.R.S.* **22**, 1951, 65-83.

STOKER, DAVID A., ed. *The correspondence of the Reverend Francis Blomefield (1705-52)*. N.R.S. **55**, 1992 (for 1990).

Campling

CAMP, ANTHONY J. 'The Campling collection for Norfolk and Suffolk', *Family tree magazine* **2**(1), 1985, 17. Describes a collection of genealogical notes at the Society of Genealogists.

Colman

COLMAN, J.J. *Bibliotheca Norfolciensis: a catalogue of the writings of Norfolk men and of works relating to the county of Norfolk in the library of Mr. J.J. Colman at Carrow Abbey, Norwich*. Norwich: Fletcher and Son, 1896.

Ketton-Cremer

GRETTON, J.R. 'A bibliography of the printed works of R.W. Ketton-Cremer M.A., D.Litt', *N.A.* **36**, 1977, 85-96.

Martin

'Bibliotheca Martiniana', *N.A.M.* **3**, 1887, 394-401. List of Norfolk and Suffolk manuscripts from an antiquary's library, now dispersed.

Rye

[RYE, WALTER.] *A catalogue of fifty of the Norfolk manuscripts in the library of Mr. Walter Rye*. Putney: [W. Rye], 1889.

STEPHEN, GEO. A. *Walter Rye: memoir, bibliography, and catalogue of his Norfolk manuscripts in the Norwich Public Libraries*. Norwich: Public Libraries Committee, 1929.

Other potentially useful bibliographic works include:

RYE, WALTER. *A short list of works relating to the biographies of Norfolk men and women, preserved in the Free Library at Norwich*. Norwich: Edward Burgess & Sons, 1908.

MANLEY, K.A. 'Sources for library history: Norfolk and Suffolk', *Library history* **8**, 1990, 145-9. The sources listed include lists of members, etc.

3. JOURNALS AND NEWSPAPERS

The most important journal for Norfolk genealogists is:

The Norfolk ancestor: journal of the Norfolk & Norwich Genealogical Society 1977- . This continues the *Norfolk and Norwich Genealogical Society journal* 1972-77, and carries extensive information on the interests of society members, thus enabling you to make contact with others who may be researching your own lines. It is required reading for every Norfolk genealogist.

For Norfolk heraldry, see:

The Norfolk standard. [ ]: Norfolk Heraldry Society, 1976-83.

Norfolk heraldry: the journal of the Norfolk Heraldry Society. Norwich: the Society, 1991-

Many original sources, indexes, etc., have been published by the *Norfolk Record Society* who issue an annual volume. Those likely to be of relevance to the genealogist are listed in the appropriate place below.

The most important—and oldest—historical journal for Norfolk is:

Norfolk archaeology, or, miscellaneous tracts relating to the antiquities of the county of Norfolk. Norwich: Norfolk and Norwich Archaeological Society, 1847-

This is indexed in:

MANNING, C.R. *A general index to the first ten volumes of Norfolk Archaeology ... 1846-1890.* Norwich: Agas Goose, 1891.

OLORENSHAW, JOHN. *A general index to vols. XI-XX of Norfolk Archaeology ...* Norwich: Goose & Son, 1928.

MORRIS, ROSE E. *A general index to vols. XXI-XXX of Norfolk Archaeology ...* Norwich: Soman-Wherry Press, 1958.

Walter Rye, the noted antiquary, edited:

The Norfolk Antiquarian miscellany. 3 + 3 vols. Norwich: Agas H. Goose, 1877-87. 2nd series, 1906-8.

A number of journals regularly published 'notes and queries', although all have now ceased publication. The most important was:

The East Anglian, or, notes and queries on subjects connected with the counties of Suffolk, Cambridge, Essex and Norfolk. 4 + 13 vols. Lowestoft: S. Tymms; London: Whitaker & Co., 1858-71. New series, 1885-1910. Each volume has its own index to persons, places and subjects, except that only subjects are indexed from N.S. 7-

The gap in publication of the *East Anglian* between 1871 and 1885 was partly filled by:

L'ESTRANGE, JOHN. *Eastern Counties Collectanea, being notes and queries on subjects relating to the counties of Norfolk, Suffolk, Essex and Cambridge.* Norwich: Thomas R. Tallack, 1872-3.

See also:

East Anglian miscellany upon matters of history, genealogy, archaeology, folk-lore, literature, etc., relating to East Anglia. Ipswich: East Anglian Daily Times, 1907-58. An index is provided in each annual volume.

East Anglian magazine. Ipswich: East Anglian Magazine, 1935-. This is indexed in:

MOLLARD, T. *Index to the East Anglian Magazine, July 1935 (issue no.1) to December 1960.* Ipswich: Library Association (Eastern Branch), 1968.

Fenland notes & queries: a quarterly antiquarian journal for the Fenland, in the counties of Huntingdon, Cambridge, Lincoln, Northampton, Norfolk and Suffolk. 7 vols. Peterborough: Geo. C. Custer, 1889-1909.

Norfolk & Norwich notes & queries, upon matters of history, genealogy, archaeology, folk-lore, literature, &c., relating to the county and city ... Norwich: Norfolk Chronicle, 1896-1906. Irregular. Reprinted articles from the *Norfolk Chronicle*. Includes much of interest to the antiquary, but only a small amount of genealogical information.

Newspapers are an important source of genealogical information—especially their notices of births, marriages and deaths. For a full listing of surviving newspapers, with locations, see:

GORDON, RUTH. *Newsplan: report of the Newsplan project in the East Midlands, April 1987-July 1988.* British Library, 1989. Also covers Cambridgeshire, Derbyshire, Leicestershire, Lincolnshire, Northamptonshire, Nottinghamshire and Suffolk.

For Janice Simons' extracts of marriage and death notices from the *Lynn Advertiser*, etc., see below, section 8.

See also:

MACKIE, CHARLES. *Norfolk annals: a chronological record of remarkable events in the nineteenth century (compiled from the files of the Norfolk Chronicle).* 2 vols. Norwich: Norfolk Chronicle, 1901. Includes many death notices.

4. NAMES

What is the meaning of that surname? And where did it come from? The origins of East Anglian surnames has been treated fully, and much valuable information is contained in:

MCKINLEY, RICHARD. *Norfolk and Suffolk surnames in the middle ages.* English surnames series **2**, Phillimore, 1975.

See also:

MCKINLEY, R.A. *Norfolk surnames in the sixteenth century.* University of Leicester Dept of English Local History occasional paper, 2nd series **2**. Leicester: Leicester University Press, 1969.

CARTHEW, G.A. *The origin of family or sur-names, with special reference to those of the inhabitants of East Dereham in the county of Norfolk.* Norwich: Agas H. Goose & Co., [1883]. Includes lists of surnames.

RYE, W. 'Personal christian or forenames which occur in the feet of fines for Norfolk, Suffolk, Cambridge, Lincoln and Essex from 1189-1216', in his *Norfolk essays* **3**, 1926, 208-34.

5. HERALDIC VISITATIONS AND PEDIGREE COLLECTIONS

In the sixteenth and seventeenth centuries, the heralds undertook 'visitations' of the counties in order to determine the right of gentry to bear heraldic arms. One consequence of this activity was the compilation of pedigrees of most of the leading gentry. These visitation pedigrees continue to be major sources of genealogical information, and many have been published. For Norfolk, see:

RYE, WALTER, ed. *The visitacion of Norffolk made and taken by William Harvey, Clarencieux King of Arms, anno 1563, enlarged with another visitacion made by Clarenceux Cooke, with many other descents; as also the vissitation made by John Raven, Richmond, anno 1613.* Harleian Society **32**, 1891.

DASHWOOD, G.H., et al, eds. *The visitation of Norfolk in the year 1563, taken by William Harvey, Clarenceux King of Arms, from Harleian mss. in the British Museum ...* 2 vols. Norwich: Miller and Leavins, for the Norfolk and Norwich Archaeological Society, 1878-95. Issued with *Norfolk archaeology.* 2nd vol. edited by W.E.G.L. Bulwer.

HART, RICHARD. 'Analysis of the Harleian manuscript Cod.4756 (bound up with 1101 and 5823 ...', *N.A.* **3**, 1852, 40-51. See also **4**, 1855, 292-5. Lists pedigrees in the visitation of 1563.

CLARKE, A.W. HUGHES, & CAMPLING, ARTHUR, eds. *The visitation of Norfolk, anno domini 1664 made by Sir Edward Bysshe, knt., Clarenceux king of arms.* 2 vols. Harleian Society **85-6**, 1933-4. Also published as N.R.S. **4-5**, 1934. See also N.R.S. **27**, 1956, 59-82, for extensive observations and comments by G.H. Holley.

This supersedes:

ATHILL, C.H. *An index to the visitation of Norfolk made A.D. 1664.* Ipswich: Pawsey & Hayes, 1885. Reprinted from *East Anglian* N.S. **1**, 1885-6, 20-21, 45-6, 52, 73-4 & 87-8.

Disclaimers at visitations are listed in:

HAMOND, A. 'Norfolk disclaimers, 1664', *N.Anc.* **3**(10), 1985, 145-7.

For surviving visitation families, see:

SAYER, M.J. 'Surviving Norfolk and Suffolk visitation families', *Genealogists magazine* **18**, 1975-6, 343-7. See also **19**, 1977-8, 20.

A general discussion of Norfolk visitations is provided by:

SAYER, M.J. 'Norfolk visitation families: a short social structure', *N.A.* **36**, 1977, 176-82. See also **37**, 1980, 319-20 and **38**, 1983, 193.

Many other collections and indexes of pedigrees have been published. They are listed here in order of the date of publication.

RYE, WALTER. *An index to Norfolk pedigrees.* Norwich: A.H. Goose, 1896. Includes continuation of *Index to Norfolk topography,* and indexes both published and manuscript material.

[CRISP, F.A., ed.] *Fragmenta Genealogica, Vol.ix.* F.A. Crisp, 1903. This volume consists of East Anglian pedigrees, mainly Norfolk and Suffolk.

RYE, WALTER. *Norfolk families.* 2 vols. Norwich: Goose and Son, 1911-13. Numerous brief descents, indexed in: NOWELL, CHARLES. *Index nominum, being an index of Christian names and surnames mentioned in Walter Rye's Norfolk families.* Norwich: Roberts & Co., 1915.

CAMPLING, ARTHUR. *East Anglian pedigrees.* 2 vols. Harleian Society publications **91 & 97,** 1937-45. Also published as N.R.S. **13,** 1940. Covers Norfolk and Suffolk; excludes most visitation pedigrees; mainly yeoman families.

PALGRAVE-MOORE, PATRICK. *A selection of revised and unpublished Norfolk pedigree.* Norfolk genealogy **6, 8, 13, 17 & 22,** 1974-90. Vol. 6 co-authored by M.J. Sayer.

SAYER, MICHAEL. *Eynsford families, 1550-1700.* Norfolk genealogy **4,** 1972. Many brief family histories.

6. GENEALOGICAL DIRECTORIES, BIOGRAPHICAL DICTIONARIES AND OCCUPATIONAL SOURCES

One of the most useful sources of genealogical information are the directories of members interests published by family history societies. These provide the names and addresses of researchers, together with the names of families they are researching. If your surname is listed, maybe someone has already done much of the work! Or at least you may be able to share the labour. For Norfolk, see:

Norfolk families: a list of Norfolk & Norwich Genealogical Society members and the family names they are researching. 4th ed. Norwich: the Society, 1989.

PERKINS, JOHN. *East Anglian families: directory 2.* Stanton: Federation of Family History Societies, 1992.

Biographical dictionaries provide brief biographical information on the individuals listed. Innumerable such dictionaries exist, and are invaluable to the genealogist. To identify them, consult the works listed in *English genealogy: an introductory bibliography.* Some are listed in *Occupational sources for genealogists.* Norfolk biographical dictionaries include:

Norfolk, Suffolk and Cambridgeshire leaders, social and political. Exeter: Pollard, [1900].

GASKELL, ERNEST. *Norfolk leaders, social and political.* Queenhithe Press, [1907].

PIKE, W.T., & HUSSEY, F. *Norfolk and Suffolk in East Anglia: contemporary biographies.* Brighton: W.T. Pike, 1911.

PIKE, W.T. *East Anglia in the twentieth century: contemporary biographies.* Brighton: W.T. Pike & Co., 1912. Suffolk and Norfolk.

HOPPER, E.C. *Norfolk and Suffolk in East Anglia in the twentieth century: contemporary biographies.* Brighton: W.T. Pike & Co., 1912.

Cox's county who's who series: Norfolk, Suffolk and Cambridgeshire, 1912. Horace Cox, 1912.

Who's who in Norfolk. Worcester: Ebenezer Baylis and Son, 1935.

Social register of the county of Norfolk. Social Registers, [1938].

Who's who in Norwich. Pullman biographical series. Pullman Press, 1961.

The works so far listed here were written for the contemporaries of the biographees. Works dealing with historical figures include:

Genealogical Directories etc. *continued*

Lives of eminent and remarkable characters, born or long resident in the counties of Essex, Suffolk and Norfolk. Longmans, Hurst, Rees, Orme & Brown, 1820.

PRESS, C.A. MANNING. *Norfolk notabilities: a portrait gallery.* Jarrold & Sons, 1893.

SMITH-DAMPIER, J.L. *East Anglian worthies.* Oxford: Basil Blackwell, 1949. 200 biographical sketches, Norfolk and Suffolk.

JEWSON, CHARLES B. *People of medieval Norwich.* Norwich: Jarrold & Sons, [1956]. Biographies of eminent persons.

BLAKE, WILLIAM J. 'Fuller's list of Norfolk gentry', *N.A.* **32**, 1961, 261-91. List of 374 Norfolk gentry, 1434, from Fuller's *Worthies of England.*

There are many works offering biographical information on persons with a particular occupation or status. These are listed here. For clergymen, see section 14; for government officials, section 16; for teachers and students, section 18.

Apothecaries

WHITTET, T. DOUGLAS. 'Norfolk apothecaries' tokens and their issuers', *N.A.* **40**, 1989, 100-109. Includes biographical notes.

Apprentices

RISING, WINIFRED M., & MILLICAN, PERCY, eds. *An index of Norwich apprentices enrolled with the Norwich Assembly, Henry VII-George II.* N.R.S. **29**, 1959.

RUTLEDGE, PAUL. *A calendar of Great Yarmouth enrolled apprenticeship indentures, 1563-1665.* Norfolk genealogy **11**, 1979.

GOODMAN, W.L. 'Woodworking apprentices and their tools in Bristol, Norwich, Great Yarmouth and Southampton, 1535-1650', *Industrial archaeology* **9**, 1972, 376-411 & 447. Gives some names.

Architects

BAGGS, A. PAGET. 'Norfolk architects, 1660-1840', *N.A.* **32**, 1961, 236-46. List with brief biographical notes.

NORFOLK AND NORWICH ASSOCIATION OF ARCHITECTS. *Year book.* Norwich: the Association, 1931-8, 1944-. Includes list of members.

Artists

DAY, HAROLD A.E. *East Anglian painters.* 3 vols. Eastbourne: Eastbourne Fine Art, 1968-9. Covers Essex, Suffolk and Norfolk; includes biographical notes.

Artists *continued*

STEPHEN, GEO. A. *Norfolk artists: an annotated catalogue of the books, pamphlets and articles relating to deceased Norfolk artists in the Norwich Public Library.* Norfolk celebrities **2**. Norwich: Public Library Committee, 1915.

RAJNAL, M. 'The members of the Norwich Society of Artists, 1805-1833', *N.A.* **34**, 1969, 429-33. Includes folded list.

RAJNAL, M. 'Exhibitors with the Norwich Society of Artists, 1805-1833', *N.A.* **35**, 1973, 233-58.

Norfolk and Norwich Arts Circle, 1885-1985: a history of the Circle, and the Centenary Exhibition. [Norwich]: the Circle, 1985. Includes list of exhibiting members.

TILLYARD, VIRGINIA. 'Painters in sixteenth and seventeenth century Norwich', *N.A.* **37**, 1980, 315-9. Notes on sources.

Barber Surgeons

WILLIAMS, CHARLES. *The masters, wardens and assistants of the Gild of Barber-Surgeons of Norwich from the year 1439 to 1723.* 2nd series. Norwich: Jarrold, 1900.

Beggars

CLARKE, BASIL. 'Norfolk licences to beg: an unpublished collection', *N.A.* **35**, 1973, 327-34. See also 510-11. Issued mainly by the Bishop of Norwich.

Bell Founders

CATTERMOLE, PAUL. *Church bells and bell-ringing: a Norfolk profile.* Woodbridge: Boydell Press, 1990. Includes chapter on bell founders.

MANDER, R.P. 'Medieval bell-founders of Norfolk and Suffolk', *East Anglian magazine* **8**, 1949, 665-70. Brief note.

Book Subscribers

H., L.J. 'East Anglian list, 1737', *E.A.M.* **1919**, 1, 4, 6, 8, 10, 14, 15-16, 18, 20-21, 22-3, 24, 29-30, 32, 33-4, 36 & 37-8. See also 54. List of subscribers to a book, from Norfolk and Suffolk.

Book Trades

FARRELL, FRANK J. *Yarmouth printing and printers.* Great Yarmouth: Jarrold & Sons, 1912. Traces 18-19th c. printers.

FAWCETT, TREVOR. 'Eighteenth-century Norfolk book-sellers: a survey and register', *Transactions of the Cambridge Bibliographical Society* **6**, 1973, 1-18. Includes list with brief biographical notes.

Genealogical Directories etc. continued

Book Trades *continued*

STOKER, DAVID. 'The Norwich book trades before 1800', *Transactions of the Cambridge Bibliographical Society* 8(1), 1981, 79-125. Extensive list of stationers, booksellers, printers, bookbinders, paper makers and newspaper proprietors, with detailed biographical notes.

Botanists

SOUTHWELL, THOS. 'Some old-time Norfolk botanists', *Transactions of the Norfolk and Norwich Naturalists Society* 8, 1904-9, 374-86. Biographical notes, 18-19th c.

Brewers

DAVIDSON, ANDREW P. *Justly celebrated ales: a directory of Norfolk brewers, 1850-1990.* New Ash Green: Brewery History Society, 1990.

Builders

WEARING, STANLEY J. *Georgian Norwich: its builders.* Norwich: Jarrold & Sons, 1926. Biographical notes on Brettingham, Ivory, Wilkins and Rawlins families.

Convicts

[MOGRIDGE, GEORGE.] *Sarah Martin: the prison visitor of Great Yarmouth: a story of a useful life.* Religious Tract Society, 1872. Makes reference to a prison journal, then in Great Yarmouth Public Library, which contains much genealogical information concerning prisoners.

See also Thieves

Fishermen

STAMMERS, MICHAEL. 'East Anglian fishermen at Liverpool', *East Coast mariner* 21, 1973, 29-30. Discussion of Board of Trade crew registers, 1890-1907.

Freemasons

AMHERST, W.A.T., & LE STRANGE, HAMON. *History of the Union Lodge, Norwich, no.52.* Norwich: Agas H. Goose, 1898. Includes lists of members, 18-19th c.

EATON, F.R. *An outline of the history of the Provincial Grand Lodge of Norfolk (1759-1959).* Norwich: Soman-Wherry Press, 1960. Gives many names, including lists of Grand Masters.

GLASIER, J.S.B., ed. *History of Philanthropic Lodge, Kings Lynn, no.107.* Kings Lynn: Geo. R. Oswell, 1911. Includes list of members, with addresses, ages, and professions.

Freemasons *continued*

LE STRANGE, HAMON. *History of freemasonry in Norfolk, 1724 to 1895.* Norwich: Agas H. Goose, 1896. Includes various lists of names.

Lodge of Sincerity, no.943: a hundred years of sincere Masonic endeavour, 1863-1963. Norwich: Modern Press, 1963. Includes list of officers.

Glass Painters

HAWARD, BIRKIN. *Nineteenth century Norfolk stained glass: gazetteer, directory, an account of Norfolk stained glass painters.* Norwich: Geo. Books/Centre of East Anglian Studies, 1984. Includes biographical information on stained glass painters.

Goldsmiths

BARRETT, GEOFFREY N. *Norwich silver and its marks, 1565-1702. The Goldsmiths of Norwich, 1141-1750.* Norwich: Wensum Press, 1981. Lists goldsmiths, with biographical details.

LEVINE, GEORGE. 'Norwich goldsmiths' marks', *N.A.* 3, 1969, 293-302. Discussions of 37 marks, identifying a number of them.

HOPE, R.C. 'English goldsmiths', *Reliquary* N.S. 2, 1888, 216-23; 3, 1889, 31-40, 74-88, 159-67 & 241-5; 4, 1890, 24-34. Lists goldsmiths in a number of towns, including Norwich.

Innkeepers

THOMPSON, LEONARD P. *Norwich inns.* Ipswich: W.E. Harrison & Sons, 1947. Includes many names of innkeepers, etc.

Lawyers

COZENS-HARDY, BASIL. 'Norfolk lawyers', *N.A.* 33, 1965, 266-97. See also 514. Biographical notes arranged by parish.

Medics

KNIGHTS, M. 'Physicians and surgeons in the 16th, 17th and 18th centuries', *Eastern Counties Collectanea* 1872/3, 247-54 & 270-71.

VERTUE, F.H. 'List of medical men living in 1728, residing in Cambridge, Suffolk and Norfolk', *East Anglian* N.S. 2, 1887-8, 10-11.

Millers

APLING, HARRY. *Norfolk corn windmills.* Norwich: Norfolk Windmills Trust, 1984. Gives names of many millers, owners, etc.

Painters

See Artists

Paper Makers

STOKER, DAVID. 'The early history of paper-making in Norfolk', *N.A.* **36**, 1977, 241-52. Traces descents of paper-mills.

See also Book Trades

Pipe Makers

ATKIN, SUSANNE. 'The clay pipe-making industry in Norfolk', *N.A.* **39**, 1986, 118-49. Includes a list.

KARSHNER, MARY. 'The tobacco clay pipe making industry in Norwich', in DAVEY, PETER, ed. *The archaeology of the clay tobacco pipe, 1: Britain: the Midlands, and Eastern England.* B.A.R. British series **63**, 1979, 295-352. Includes extensive list of pipe makers, with probate inventory of Lawrence Mosely, 1691.

OSWALD, ADRIAN. 'Identifiable pipes of the Norwich makers', in DAVEY, PETER, ed. *The archaeology of the clay tobacco pipe, 1: Britain: the Midlands and Eastern England.* B.A.R. British series **63**, 1979, 353-9. Includes some names.

Policy Holders

BELLINGER, ROGER. 'The Amicable Society for a Perpetual Assurance Office', *N.Anc.* **3**(4), 1984, 47-51. Includes list of Norfolk policy holders, 1706/7.

Postmasters

SUSSEX, V.J. *The Norwich Post Office, 1568-1980: its postmasters, services and postal markings.* Postal history of East Anglia **7**. Coggeshall: East Anglian Postal History Study Centre, 1980. Includes list of postmasters from 1649 to 1980.

Printers

See Book Trades

Railway Passengers

PEARCE, D.H. 'The Thorpe railway accident, 1875, *N.Anc.* **3**(1), 1983, 3-4. Includes list of 250 people involves.

Seamen

COZENS-HARDY, BASIL. 'Havens in North Norfolk', *N.A.* **35**, 1973, 356-63. Includes extracts from court rolls, giving some names of seamen.

Shipbuilders

MALSTER, R. 'Shipbuilders of Yarmouth', *Norfolk sailor* **8**, 1964, 2-8. 19th c. General discussion; some names.

Shipbuilders *continued*

MALTSTER, R.W. 'The wherry builders', *East Coast mariner* **17**, 1970, 24-31. General discussion; some names.

Soldiers, Militiamen and Volunteers

Many men of Norfolk served in the army or the militia, and much information on them is available in the various regimental histories, honour rolls, etc., which have been published. These cannot all be listed here. The following works all include lists of names or other information of direct genealogical value, and are arranged in rough chronological order. General histories without such information are excluded.

RYE, WALTER. *A list of Norfolk fighting men from the Norman period to the reign of Queen Victoria.* Rye's Norfolk handlists, 1st series **5**. Norwich: Roberts & Co., 1916. Brief biographical notes on many soldiers.

DAVIES, GODFREY. 'The army of the Eastern Association, 1644-5', *English historical review* **46**, 1931, 88-96. Includes list of Parliamentary officers.

PETRE, F. LORAINE. *The history of the Norfolk Regiment, 1685-1918.* 2 vols. Norwich: Jarrold & Sons, 1924-6. Includes list of officers killed, 1914-18, detailed listing of sources, etc.

HARVEY, SIR CHARLES. *History of the 4th Battalion, Norfolk Regiment (late East Norfolk Militia).* Jarrold & Sons, 1899. Includes list of officers, 1759-1898.

HARVEY, J.R. *Records of the Norfolk Yeomanry Cavalry, to which is added, The Fencible and Provisional Cavalry of the same county from 1780 to 1908 ...* Jarrold & Sons, 1908. Includes various lists.

BASTIN, JEREMY. *Norfolk yeomanry in peace and war, 1782-1961.* Fakenham: Iceni Press, 1986. Includes rolls of honour for 1914-18 and 1939-45.

JONES, HONOR. 'Western Regiment of Norfolk Militia', *N.Anc.* **4**(6), 1987, 96-7. Lists deserters, with ages, descriptions, homes, etc., and names of men for whom they served as substitutes in 1803; from *Norwich Mercury.* See also:

'Army of the Reserve deserted from Norwich', *N.Anc.* **3**(2), 1983, 26.

GLIDDON, GERALD, ed. *Norfolk and Suffolk in the Great War.* Norwich: Gliddon Books, 1988. Includes many names.

Soldiers, Militiamen and Volunteers *continued*

IMPERIAL WAR GRAVES COMMISSION. *The war dead of the Commonwealth: the register of the names of those who fell in the Great War and are buried in cemeteries and churchyards in the administrative county of Norfolk, 1914-1918.* Maidenhead: Commonwealth War Graves Commission, 1989.

Norfolk roll of honour 1914-18: list of men from Norfolk parishes who fell in the Great War. [Norwich]: Gliddon, c.1988. Originally published [Norwich]: Norfolk news, 1920.

Norwich roll of honour of citizens who fell in the Great War, 1914-19. Norwich: London and Norwich Press for Norwich Corporation, 1924.

Soldiers died in the Great War 1914-1918, pt.14: The Norfolk Regiment. H.M.S.O., 1921. Reprinted Chippenham: Picton, 1988.

IMPERIAL WAR GRAVES COMMISSION. *Roll of honour of the civilian war dead 1939-1945. Norfolk: Great Yarmouth, Norwich, Blofield, and Flegg, Cromer.* The Commission, [1945].

WILSON, H.M., & HOLDEN, H.R., eds. *History of the Royal Norfolk Regiment (9), 1st Battalion, in the Korean War.* [Norwich?]: [ ], 1952. Includes roster.

Surveyors

EDEN, PETER. 'Land surveyors in Norfolk, 1550-1850', *N.A.* **35**, 1973, 474-82; **36**, 1977, 119-48. Includes a list, with biographical notes.

Swan Owners

Swan owners are listed in three works:

MINET, WILLIAM. 'Two early seventeenth-century rolls of Norfolk swan-marks', *Proceedings of the Society of Antiquaries of London* 2nd series **20**, 1903-5, 276-86.

TICEHURST, N.F. 'The swan roll in the Norwich Castle Museum', *Transactions of the Norfolk and Norwich Naturalists Society* **12**, 1924-9, 17-24.

TICEHURST, N.F. 'The swan-marks of East Norfolk', *Transactions of the Norfolk and Norwich Naturalists Society* **12**, 1924-9, 424-60. For West Norfolk, see 581-630.

Theatre Proprietors

ESHLEMAN, DOROTHY H., ed. *The committee books of the Theatre Royal, Norwich, 1768-1825.* Society for Theatre Research, 1970. Includes various lists of names of persons connected with the theatre—especially the proprietors.

Thieves

HARROD, HENRY. 'Extracts from the assize and plea rolls of the thirteenth century about Norwich thieves, &c.', *N.A.* **74**, 1872, 263-75.

HANAWALT, BARBARA, ed. *Crime in East Anglia in the fourteenth century: Norfolk gaol delivery rolls, 1307-1316.* N.R.S. **44**, 1976. Names of criminals, with particulars of crime, and names of accusers.

See also Convicts

Tradesmen

EWING, WILLIAM C. 'Notices of the Norwich merchant marks', *N.A.* **3**, 1852, 177-228. Many names of traders, medieval-16th c.

GURNEY-READ, JOYCE. *Trades and industries of Norwich.* Norwich: Gliddon Books, 1988. Brief histories of local businesses.

In an age when currency was in short supply, many tradesmen issued tokens. These tokens usually give their names and residences, and those for Norfolk have been the subject of two studies, which provide information of potential genealogical value. See:

TILLETT, E.A. *The tokens of Norfolk, issued in the seventeenth, eighteenth and nineteenth centuries, together with notices of some of the issuers.* Norwich: Agas H. Goose, 1882. Originally published in *Eastern Counties Collectanea.*

GOLDING, C. 'East Anglian tradesmen's tokens: Norfolk', *East Anglian* **4**, 1869, 130-32, 157-60, 231-2 & 259.

7. FAMILY HISTORIES, PEDIGREES, ETC.

Works on the history of particular families are listed here. An attempt has been made to indicate the periods covered. Biographies are not, in general, included; for them, reference must be made to the works listed in section 2 above.

Aickman

AICKMAN, DOROTHY JEAN. *John Aickman's foundery MDCCCXXVII, Kings Lynn: a fragment of Lynn history*. Cambridge: the author, 1980. History of a family business, 18-19th c.

Albini

SIMPSON, JUSTIN. 'An historical account of the families of Albini and Moubray', *East Anglian* 2, 1866, 43-7, 54-7, 69-72, 100-104, 114-7 & 137-8. See also 125. Medieval.

Ames

ROBINSON, J.A., ed. *The Ames correspondence: letters to Mary: a selection of letters written by members of the Ames family of Lakenham, Norwich, 1837-1847*. N.R.S. **31**, 1962.

Amyas

'From the register of Great Dunham, Norfolk', *Genealogist* 2, 1878, 130-31. Amyas family, 17th c., includes extracts from parish registers of Little Dunham and Litcham, with wills.

Amyot

AMYOT, T.E. 'Pedigree of the Huguenot family of Amyot', *M.G.H.* 3rd series **2**, 1898, 26-30. Of France, Norfolk and Lincolnshire, 16-19th c.

Arterton

JONES, ANN. 'The Felthorpe Artertons, 1811-1933', *N.Anc.* 4(6), 1987, 88-90.

Astley

KETTON-CREMER, R.W. *Three generations*. Privately printed, 1958. Reprinted Norfolk: Larks Press, 1992, with introduction by David Yaxley. Astley family, 17th c.

Bacon

MILLICAN, PERCY. 'The Bacons of Earlham', *N.A.* **33**, 1965, 86-93. Includes pedigree, 17-19th c.
RYE, WALTER. *The false pedigree and arms of the family of Bacon of Suffolk, the ancestors of Sir Nicholas Bacon (Lord Verulam) and of the present premier baronet, critically examined and exposed*. Norwich: Roberts & Co., 1919. 11-16th c. Also deals with the Norfolk branch of the family.

Bagge

CAMPLING, ARTHUR. 'Bagge of Shipdham, Co.Norfolk', *M.G.H.* 5th series **8**, 1932-4, 321. Pedigree, 16-19th c., also of Cockley Cley.

Bainard

LANDON, L. 'The Bainard family in Norfolk', *N.A.* **22**, 1926, 209-20. Medieval; includes pedigree.

Barker

BARRON, OSWALD. 'The gentility of Richard Barker', *Ancestor* 2, July 1902, 48-53. 16th c.
GRAZEBROOK, GEO. 'A curiosity from the Court of Star Chamber', *M.G.H.* 4th series **1**, 1906, 11-16. Complaint of Richard Barker, 1541, concerning his claim to gentility.

Barcham

BARCHAM, THOMAS. *Historical and biographical notices of the Barcham family of Norfolk from 1610 to 1853*. Reading: the author, 1857.

Barclay

BARCLAY, CHARLES W., ed. *A history of the Barclay family, with full pedigree from 1066 to 1924*. 3 vols. St.Catherine Press, 1924-34.

Barrett

See Lennard

Barritt

BARRITT, R.A. *Barritts of the Fenland*. Upminster: the author, 1970.

Bayley

LEATHER, JOHN. 'A shipbuilding family', *Norfolk sailor* **10**, 1965, 3-13 & **11**, 1966, 3-14. Bayley family, 18-19th c.

Beaufoy

RYE, WALTER. 'The alleged identity of Bishop William de Bellafago of Thetford with Bishop Herbert de Losinga of Norwich', *N.A.M.* **1**, 1877, 413-9. Includes folded pedigree of Beaufoy, 10-12th c.

Beaupre

See Bell

Bedingfeld

BEDINGFELD, KATHERINE. *The Bedingfelds of Oxburgh*. Privately printed, 1912.
POLLEN, J.H., ed. 'Bedingfeld papers', *Publications of the Catholic Record Society* 7, 1909, 1-243. See also 423-34 for genealogical supplement. Bedingfeld family of Oxburgh. Includes extracts from parish registers, monumental inscriptions, pedigree, 16-19th c., many letters, diaries, accounts, etc.

Bedingfeld *continued*

WADLEY, T.P. 'Bedingfeld: from the parish registers of Ditchingham, Norfolk', *Genealogist* **1**, 1877, 239-40. 17-18th c.

Bell

JOSSELYN, JOHN HENRY. *A genealogical account of the descendants of Sir Robert Bell, Knt., ... with a history of the illustrious ancestry of his wife Dorothy, co-heir of the ancient family of Beaupre.* Ipswich: S. & W.J. King, 1896. Essex and Norfolk; Bell, Beaupre, Hawkwood, Coggeshall, Harsyke, Doreward and Fodringhay families, 11-9th c.

Benelande

BEANLAND, A. 'The Benelandes of Rockland Tofts', *N.A.M.* 2nd series **1**, 1906, 46-7.

Berney

FELLOWES, EDMUND HORACE. *A complete roll of the descendants, living or lately living in 1910, of Thomas Berney, of Swardeston Hall, County Norfolk ...* [ ]: privately published, [1911]. Includes pedigrees, 17-20th c.

Bessey

See Gotts

Bignold

BIGNOLD, SIR ROBERT. *Five generations of the Bignold family, 1761-1947, and their connection with the Norwich Union.* B.T. Batsford, 1948. Includes pedigree, 14-20th c., showing Surrey origins.

Bigod

'The Bigod family', *N.A.M.* 2nd series **2**, 1907, 131-41. Medieval-18th c.

Blennerhassett

MORIARTY, G. ANDREWS. 'Genealogical research in England: the East Anglian Blennerhassets', *New England historical and genealogical register* **98**(3), 1944, 271-9. Includes pedigree, 14-16th c. Of Cumberland, Norfolk and Suffolk.

Blithe

BLYTH, WILLIAM. *A brief historical sketch of the ancient name and family of Blithe, Blythe, or Blyth in the counties of Warwickshire, Derbyshire & Norfolk.* Norwich: A.H. Goose, 1885.

See also Kerslake

Blofeld

B[LOFELD], T.C.B. *An account of the Blofeld family of Hoveton House in the County of Norfolk.* [ ], [1968?]. Includes pedigree, 18-20th c.

Blomefield

HAWES, T.L.M. 'Genealogy of the Reverend Francis Blomefield', *N.A.* **38**, 1983, 59-66. 16-19th c.

RYE, WALTER. 'The real pedigree of Blomefield, the author of the *History of Norfolk*', in his *Some historical essays chiefly relating to Norfolk* **3**, 1926, 205-7.

Blundeville

CAMPLING, ARTHUR. 'Blundeville of Newton Flotman and Heckingham, Co.Norfolk', *M.G.H.* 5th series **9**, 1935-7, 181-7. 12-20th c.

CAMPLING, ARTHUR. 'Thomas Blundeville of Newton Flotman, Co.Norfolk (1522-1606) author and poet, temp Elizabeth', *N.A.* **21**, 1923, 337-60. Includes pedigree 11-20th c.

Blyth

See Blithe

Boleyn

PARSONS, W.L.E. 'Some notes on the Boleyn family', *N.A.* **25**, 1935, 386-407. Includes pedigree, 13-15th c.

Bolter

BOULTER, W. CONSITT. 'Bolter of South Creake: visitation of Norfolk 1613', *M.G.H.* N.S. **1**, 1874, 25.

Booty

BOOTY, HAROLD. *The Bootys of Norfolk, Suffolk, Kent and Devonshire.* Privately printed, 1983. Includes pedigree, 16-20th c.

BOOTY, HAROLD. *Some Bootys and their forebears: a family history.* Guildford: privately printed, 1976. 16-20th c. Includes pedigrees.

Bois

BOYS, HENRY S. *Pedigree of du Bois, Boys, Boyce, etc.* ed. Guy P. Boys. [ ]: [ ], 1939. Also of Leicestershire and Lincolnshire.

Bradbrooke

BRADBROOKE, WILLIAM. *The Bradbrooke family register.* Kingston: privately printed, 1935. Medieval-20th c., also of Buckinghamshire, Middlesex, Worcestershire, etc.

Browne

CAMPLING, ARTHUR. 'Browne of Elsing, Co.Norfolk', *M.G.H.* 5th series, **9**, 1935-7, 317-21. Pedigree, 14-20th c.

Browne *continued*

CAMPLING, ARTHUR. 'Browne of Mundsley and Fulmodeston', *M.G.H.* 5th series **8**, 1932-4, 264-5. Pedigree, 17-18th c.

MILEHAM, JOHN. 'Dame Dorothy Browne and the family of Mileham of Burlingham', *N.Anc.* 2(8), 1982, 104-9. 17th c.

RYE, WALTER. 'Sir Thomas Browne, his descent and arms, and his possible family connection with the family of Dr. Dee, the mystic', in his *Some historical essays chiefly relating to Norfolk* 6, 1928, 449-534. 16-17th c.

WILLIAMS, CHARLES. 'The pedigree of Sir Thomas Browne', *N.A.* **15**, 1904, 109-13. 16-19th c., of Cheshire and Norfolk.

Buckingham

RAIMONDO, HILARY. *Our company before: a history of the Buckingham family in East Anglia and New Zealand, 1682-1982.* Kensington Park, S.A.: Hilary Raimondo, 1987. Norfolk, Suffolk and New Zealand.

MAUDSLEY, HENRY. *Notes and extracts from numerous authorities respecting the family of Bukenham or Bokenham of Norfolk and Suffolk, from A.D. 1066 to A.D. 1883, and the places of that designation in the first named county.* Privately printed, 1884.

Bulwer

See Dalling

Burney

HEMLOW, JOYCE. *A catalogue of the Burney family correspondence, 1749-1878.* New York: New York Public Library, [1971].

Burrowes

See Wiggon

Burton

See Sheppard

Buxton

RYE, WALTER. 'Buxton of Shadwell Court', *Ancestor* **6**, July 1903, 11-18. Medieval.

Call

ROMANES, CHARLES S. *The Calls of Norfolk and Suffolk: their Paston connections and descendants.* Edinburgh: T. & A. Constable, 1920. 14-20th c.

'Call: Edingthorpe registers', *M.G.H.* 3rd series **2**, 1898, 117-8. 16-18th c.

Calthorpe

CARR-CALTHROP, CHRISTOPHER WILLIAM. *Notes on the families of Calthorpe and Calthrop in the counties of Norfolk and Lincolnshire and elsewhere.* 3rd ed. Privately printed, 1933.

LEE-WARNER, JAMES. 'The Calthorps of Burnham', *N.A.* **9**, 1884, 1-19. Medieval.

LEE-WARNER, H.J. 'The Calthorps of Cockthorp', *N.A.* **9**, 1884, 153-79. Includes pedigree, 16-17th c.

Carter

HOLLWAY, MICHAEL. 'The Reverend John Carter of Mattishall, and the Wigg family of Dereham', *N.Anc.* 5(5), 1989, 101-3. 18-19th c.

Catelyn

S., F.H. 'Some notes on the family of Catelyn with extracts from the parish registers of Kirby Cane ...', *East Anglian* N.S. **10**, 1903-4, 361-4 & 376-8. 16-18th c.

Cawston

BEHRENS, LILIAN BOYS. *Echoes of the good and fallen angels, De Cawston, Norfolk.* Battle: Olivers Print Works, 1956. Medieval-20th c.

Chaucer

RYE, WALTER. 'Was Chaucer a Norfolk man?', *N.A.M.* **2**, 1883, 550-52. Medieval.

Chesney

CHESNEY, R.W.L. 'The Chesney family of Norfolk: medieval history and arms', *N.Anc.* 1(7), 1979, 87-94. Includes pedigree.

Clere

JESSOPP, AUGUSTUS. 'Pedigree of Clere of Blickling', *Genealogist* **3**, 1879, 291-4. 16-17th c., includes extracts from parish registers.

RYE, WALTER. 'The De Clares of Clare in Suffolk (Earls of Gloucester) and the De Cleres of Ormesby and Stokesby in Norfolk', *Genealogist* N.S. **37**, 1921, 169-73. 12-13th c.

RYE, WALTER. 'Doubtful Norfolk pedigree, no.IV: Clere', *Genealogist* **4**, 1880, 99-102. 11-14th c.

Coggeshall

See Bell

Coke

PARKER, R.A.C. *Coke of Norfolk: a financial and agricultural study, 1707-1842.* Clarendon Press, 1975. Includes pedigree, 16-19th c.

WOOD, NEAL P. 'Coke of Holkham', *Norfolk Standard* 1(2), 1976, 26-30. 16-19th c.

Colman

COLMAN, HELEN CAROLINE. *Jeremiah James Colman: a memoir.* Chiswick Press, 1905. Includes folded pedigree, 17-20th c.

Copeman

Copeman's of Norwich. Norwich: Jarrold and Sons, 1946. History of a family business, 18-20th c.

Corbett

ENGLAND, R.M., & PALGRAVE-MOORE, P. 'A Corbett mystery', *N.Anc.* 2(8), 1982, 110-11. 17-18th c.

Corbould

POULTER, GEORGE C.B. *The Corbould genealogy.* Ipswich: W.E. Harrison & Sons for the Suffolk Institute of Archaeology, 1935. Of Suffolk, Norfolk, etc., medieval-20th c. Includes pedigrees.

Cotman

See Hooker

Cozens

See Hardy

Crabbe

RYE, WALTER. 'The poet Crabbe', *East Anglian* 2, 1866, 259. Pedigree, 18-19th c.

Crickmer

See Sheppard

Cromwell

C., G.A. 'Cromwell family: extracts from parish registers of North Elmham, Norfolk', *M.G.H.* N.S. 2, 1877, 112-3. 16th c.

Cruso

BARNARD, GEORGE W.G. 'Pedigree of the family of Cruso', *Genealogist* N.S. 18, 1902, 246-52. 17-19th c.

Cubitt

CUBITT, G.E.S. *Robert Cubitt of Bacton, Norfolk, 1713-1790, and his Cubitt descendants.* 2nd ed. Winchester: the author, 1963.

RYE, WALTER. *Collections for a history of the family of Cubitt of Norfolk.* Norwich: Samuel Miller, 1873. Reprinted from *N.A.M.* 1, 1877, 215-66. Monumental inscriptions, parish registers, etc., mainly 18-19th c., but includes list of wills from 15th c.

Curson

See Lavile

Curties

CURTIES, E.A. 'The Curties family of Norfolk', *N.Anc.* 2(2), 1980, 17-22. Includes pedigree, 16-20th c.

Dacre

See Lennard

Dade

'Dade notes', *M.G.H.* 2nd series **1**, 1886, 199-204, 240-44, 246-7, 268, 277-9, 325-8, 363-4 & 382-3; **2**, 1888, 11-12, 16, 49-51, 80 & 83-5. Dade family of Suffolk and Norfolk; includes extracts from parish registers, monumental inscriptions, wills, etc., 16-19th c.

Dagworth

CAPP, B.S. 'Sir Nicholas de Dagworth: the career of a royal servant in the fourteenth century', *N.A.* **34**, 1969, 111-18. Includes Dagworth pedigree, 13-15th c.

Dalling

SLEGG, WILLIAM BEAUMONT. *The families of Dalling and Bulwer of Wood Dalling, Norfolk.* Norwich: Goose & Son, [1943]. Includes pedigrees, 15-18th c.

Dalyson

DALISON, MRS. 'Dalyson and Tuthill: Close rolls, 34 Elizabeth part 8 (no.1412)', *M.G.H.* 3rd series **2**, 1898, 1-2. Of Lincolnshire and Norfolk, concerns marriage settlement.

Damant

DAMANT, M. 'Damant of Lammas', *N.A.M.* 2nd series **2**, 1907, 97-109. 17-19th c.

Dee

See Browne

De Lande

CASLEY, HENRY C. 'French refugees in East Anglia', *East Anlgian* N.S. **1**, 1885-6, 81-2 & 99-102. De Lande family.

Dennys

DENNY, H.L.L. 'Pedigrees of some East Anglian Dennys', *Genealogist* N.S. **38**, 1921, 15-28. Of Suffolk and Norfolk.

Donne

MANNING, CHARLES ROBERTSON. 'Pedigree of the family of Donne of Mattishall, Co.Norfolk', *M.G.H.* 3rd series **1**, 1896, 89-92. 18-19th c.

Doreward

See Bell

D'Oyly

RIVIERE, MICHAEL. 'A note on the D'Oylys of Shotesham', *N.A.* **32**, 1961, 47-9. 16-17th c.

D'Oyry

MAJOR, KATHLEEN. *The D'Oyrys of South Lincolnshire, Norfolk and Holderness, 1130-1275*. Lincoln: the author, 1984. Includes pedigrees, charters, etc.

Drury

CAMPLING, ARTHUR. *The history of the family of Drury in the counties of Suffolk and Norfolk from the Conquest*. Mitchell Hughes & Clarke, 1937. Includes pedigrees.

Duckett

C., G.A. 'Duckettiana', *Herald & genealogist* **6**, 1871, 320. Pedigree, 16-18th c.

DUCKETT, SIR G.F. *Duchetiana, or, historical and genealogical memoirs of the family of Duket, from the Conquest to the present time, in the counties of Lincoln, Westmoreland, Wilts., Cambridge and Buckinghamshire* ... J. Russell Smith, 1874. Includes notices of Windesore family.

Ellingham

ELLINGHAM, JOAN C. 'Did John Ellingham come from Blofield?', *N.Anc.* **4**(6), 1987, 92-5. Includes pedigrees, 18-20th c.

Elwyn

MORIARTY, G. ANDREWS. 'The Elwyns of Norfolk', *M.G.H.* 5th series **6**, 1926-8, 20-32. Wills, deeds, parish registers extracts, inquisitions post mortem, etc., 16-17th c.

'Elwyn of Wooddalling, Thurning, and Heigham, Co.Norfolk', *M.G.H.* 5th series **6**, 1926-8, 17-19. Pedigrees, 16-17th c.

Erpingham

RYE, WALTER. 'The Erpingham pedigree', in his *Some historical essays chiefly relating to Norfolk* **2**, 1926, 167-84.

Ewen

EWEN, C. L'ESTRANGE. *The families of Ewen of East Anglia and the Fenland*. Mitchell Hughes & Clarke, 1928. Of Suffolk, Essex, Cambridgeshire, Norfolk, etc., 11-20th c. Includes pedigrees, wills, parish register extracts, etc.

Eyre

HOLT, T.G. 'A note on Bury's Hall in Norfolk', *Recusant history* **18**, 1986-7, 440-43. Eyre family, 17-18th c.

Fellowes

FELLOWES, EDMUND HORACE. *The family and descendants of William Fellowes of Eggesford*. Windsor: Oxley & Son, 1910. Eggesford, Devon. The family was also of Norfolk, 17-19th c.

Fiske

FFISKE, HENRY. *The Fiske family papers*. Norwich: Fletcher & Son, 1902. Includes pedigrees, 13-19th c.

Fodringhay

See Bell

Forster

EDDINGTON, ARTHUR J. 'The Forsters of Bradpole and Norwich', *Friends quarterly examiner* **1933**, 349-62. Bradpole, Dorset; 18-19th c.

Frere

FRERE, HORACE, & HOWARD, ARTHUR, eds. *Pedigree of the family of Frere, of Roydon in Norfolk, and Finningham in Suffolk*. [ ]: [ ], 1899. 13-19th c.

FRERE, JASPER GRAY. *Frere of Suffolk and Norfolk from 1275-1965*. Yateley: the author, 1965. Includes many brief Frere biographies.

Fynes

See Lennard

Fysh

FYSH, J.P.G., & FYSH, A.V.G.A. 'A Fysh family in London and further afield', *N.Anc.* **2**(1), 1980, 3-9. 19-20th c.

FYSH, J.P.G., & FYSH, A.V.G.A. 'Fysh: the varying fortunes of a 19th century family', *N.Anc.* **1**(8), 1979, 106-10.

FYSH, J.P.G., & FYSH, A.V.G.A. 'Goodbye, Norfolk, I must leave you', *N.Anc.* **3**(7), 1984, 94-6. Fysh family; includes pedigree, 18-19th c.

FYSH, J.P.G., & FYSH, A.V.G.A. 'Some notes on the Fysh family of Ringstead', *N.Anc.* **4**(9), 1987, 146-8. 18th c.

Gawdy

JEAYES, ISAAC HERBERT. *Letters of Philip Gawdy of West Harling, Norfolk and of London, to various members of his family, 1579-1616*. Roxburgh Club **9**. J.B. Nichols and Sons, 1906. Includes pedigree, 16-17th c.

MILLICAN, PERCY. *The Gawdys of Norfolk and Suffolk*. Norwich: A.H. Goose, 1939. Reprinted from *N.A.* **26**, 1938, 335-90 & **27**, 1939, 31-93. 16-17th c., includes pedigrees and wills, etc.

Gawdy *continued*

RYE, WALTER. *Report on the manuscripts of the family of Gawdy, formerly of Norfolk.* C.4576. H.M.S.O., 1885. Historical Manuscripts Commission report. Mainly letters, 16-17th c., relating to Gawdy, Knyvet, Hobart, Hare, and Le Neve families.

Gawsell

DASHWOOD, G.H. 'Notes on the Gawsell pedigree', *N.A.* **5**, 1860, 277-86.

Gibson

See Young

Gilman

AMES, C.L. *The story of the Gilmans and a Gilman genealogy of the descendants of Edward Gilman of Hingham, England, 1550-1950.* Yakima, Washington: [ ], [1950].

Goggs

FONE, J.F. 'Anecdotes of the Goggs family, Norfolk farmers', *N.Anc.* **3**(6), 88-90. 16-19th c.

Goodbody

ROYALL, ARTHUR. 'The Goodbodys of Norfolk', *N.Anc.* **5**(1), 1988, 5-7. Medieval-20th c.

Goodricke

GOODRICKE, CHARLES ALFRED, ed. *History of the Goodricke family.* Hazell, Watson & Viney, 1885. Of Lincolnshire, Suffolk, Cambridgeshire, Norfolk and Yorkshire; includes pedigrees, 15-19th c.

Goodwin

HUGHES, MARK H. 'Twins in a Norwich family', *Genealogists magazine* **16**, 1970, 218-22. Goodwin family, 18-19th c.

GOODWYN, HENRY WILLIAM. *The Goodwyns of Lynn Regis, Norfolk.* Lymington: E. King, 1876. See also Warde

Gotts

GOTTS, IAN. 'At sea: a story of two Hemsby families', *N.Anc.* **5**(3), 1988, 52-4. Gotts and Bessey families; includes pedigree, 19-20th c.

GOTTS, IAN. 'What price the red tyrant? A rural ride round East Ruston', *N.Anc.* **6**(4), 1991, 113-21. Gotts family; includes extracts from the census, 1841-71.

Gournay

See Gurnay

Greenwood

GREENWOOD, I.J. 'Greenwood of Norwich', *M.G.H.* 2nd series **5**, 1894, 253-4. 16-17th c.

Gresham

LEVESON-GOWER, GRANVILLE. 'Gresham: genealogical memoranda relating to the family of Gresham', *M.G.H.* N.S. **1**, 1874, 373-5, 401-7 & 429-36. Extracts from parish registers in many counties, including Norfolk; also dispensations, marriage allegations, monumental inscriptions, etc.

LEVESON-GOWER, GRANVILLE. 'Genealogical memoranda relating to the Gresham family', *M.G.H.* **2**, 1876, 311-6. Norfolk and London; grants of arms and pedigrees, 15-17th c.

'Gresham de Gresham et de Holte in Norff', *M.G.H.* N.S. **4**, 1884, 80-81 & 90-91. 15-17th c.

'Pedigree of Gresham: pedigree A: Gresham of Walsingham Parva, Co.Norf', *M.G.H.* N.S. **4**, 1884, 262-3. Great Walsingham; 16-17th c.

'Pedigree of Gresham of Holt, Co.Norfolk, and of Titsey and Limpsfield, Co.Surrey', *M.G.H.* N.S. **4**, 1884, 251-6. 14-16th c.

Grimston

RYE, WALTER. 'The Grimston family: a query as to the alleged Yorkshire descent', in his *Some historical essays chiefly relating to Norfolk* **5**, 1927, 392-405. Medieval.

Grimwood

See Master

Gurdon

GURDON, W.B., ed. 'The Gurdon papers', *East Anglian* N.S. **4**, 1891-2, 337-9, 353-8, 369-73; **5**, 1893-4, passim. Gurdon family, 17-18th c.

Gurney

ANDERSON, VERILY. *Friends and relations: three centuries of Quaker families.* Hodder & Stoughton, 1980. Gurney family, 16-19th c.

ANDERSON, VERILY. *The Northrepps grandchildren.* Hodder & Stoughton, 1968. Reprinted Mallard Reprints, 1979. Gurney family.

EDDINGTON, ARTHUR J. 'The Gurney manuscripts', *Journal of the Friends Historical Society* **29**, 1932, 31-40; **30**, 1933, 22-7. 18-19th c. letters.

EDDINGTON, A.J., ET AL. *List and index of Gurney mss. at the Friends House Library, London.* List and Index Society, special series **6**, 1973. Lists letters and papers of the Gurney family, 1750-1850; includes much material on Quaker affairs.

Gurney *continued*

EDWARDS, J.K. 'The Gurneys and the Norwich clothing trade in the eighteenth century', *Journal of the Friends Historical Society* **50**, 1962-4, 134-52. Includes pedigree.

GURNEY, DANIEL. *The record of the house of Gournay*. 3 vols. John Bowyer Nichols & John Gough Nichols, 1848. Of West Barsham, Keswick and Somerset. Includes many pedigrees, deeds, wills, etc., medieval-19th c.

GURNEY, DANIEL. *Supplement to the record of the house of Gurney*. Kings Lynn: Thew & Son, 1858. Medieval-17th c., includes many extracts from the public records, etc.

HANNAY, JAMES. *Three hundred years of a Norman house: the barons of Gournay from the tenth to the thirteenth centuries*. Tinsley Brothers, 1867.

HARE, AUGUSTUS J.C. *The Gurneys of Earlham*. 2 vols. George Allen, 1895. 17-19th c.

HODGKIN, T. 'The Gurneys as bankers', *Friends quarterly examiner* **35**, 1901, 341-70.

RYE, W. 'The Gurneys of Norwich', *N.A.M.* 2nd series **2**, 1907, 68-96. 16-18th c.

Gwyn

RYE, WALTER. 'Mantelpiece at Fakenham', *N.A.* **14**, 1901, 341-3. Includes pedigree of Gwyn, 16-19th c.

Gyney

'Gyney of Haveringland and Dilham, Co.Norfolk', *M.G.H.* 5th series **10**, 1938, 108-9. Pedigree, 12-15th c.

Hall

See Rainsford

Hammond

PEARSON, W.C. 'Hammond, Kenton and Langham families, Co.Norfolk', *East Anglian* N.S. **5**, 1893-4, 238. Pedigree, 18-19th c.

Hardy

COZENS-HARDY, B., ed. 'Mary Hardy's diary. N.R.S. **37**, 1968. Covers 1773-1809; includes outline pedigrees of Raven, Hardy and Cozens, 18-19th c.

Hare

'Family of Hare', *East Anglian* **1**, 1864, 56-8. 16-17th c.

See also Gawdy

Harrison

MILLER, S. 'The Harrison family bible', *N.Anc.* **5**(1), 1988, 11. 18-19th c.

Harsyke

See Bell

Hart

See Rainsford

Haslewood

BARRETT, G.N. 'The Haslewood family of Norwich goldsmiths', *N.A.* **33**, 1965, 318-20. 17-18th c.

Hawkwood

See Bell

Hawtayne

See Master

Hayden

HAYDEN, W.B. *The Haydens in England and America: a fragment of family history*. James Speirs, 1877. Of Norfolk, Watford, Devon and the U.S.A. 13-19th c.

Henicames

F., E. 'Family of Henicames or Hingham, of Suffolk and Norfolk', *E.A.M.* **1907**, 27, 33, 40, 44-5 & 47-8. 17-18th c., includes wills and deeds.

Hernes

MARSHALL, GEORGE W. 'Pedigree of the Hernes of Tibbenham, Co.Norfolk', *East Anglian* **4**, 1871, 123-5. 17th c.

Heyward

ROWE, A.F. 'Errors in a visitation pedigree', *Genealogists magazine* **6**, 1932-4, 548-9. Concerns 17th c. Heyward family.

Hingham

See Henicames

Hoare

See Hore

Hobart

BULWER, BRIG-GENERAL. 'The Hobarts of Hales Hall', *N.A.* **12**, 1895, 158-63. 14-18th c.

See also Gawdy

Hooker

ALLAN, MEA. *The Hookers of Kew, 1785-1911*. Michael Joseph, 1967. Also of Great Yarmouth and Suffolk, includes pedigree, 17-20th c., with Vincent and Cotman pedigrees, 18-19th c.

Hore

HOARE, EDWARD. *Some account of the early history and genealogy, with pedigrees from 1330 unbroken to the present time, of the families of Hore and Hoare, with all their branches.* A.R. Smith, 1883.

Horth

HORTH, R.A. 'An undistinguished family, 1457-1980', *N.Anc.* 6(3), 1991, 77-9. Horth family.

HORTH, RON. 'The migration of Horths from Norwich/Norfolk (a survey of the distribution of the surname, 1275-1990)', *N.Anc.* 6(6), 1992, 190-92.

Howard

BRENAN, GERALD, & STATHAM, EDWARD PHILLIPS. *The house of Howard.* 2 vols. Hutchinson & Co., 1907. Includes folded pedigrees, medieval-20th c.

COLLIER, J. PAYNE, ed. *Household books of John Duke of Norfolk and Thomas Earl of Surrey, from the original manuscripts in the library of the Society of Antiquaries, London.* William Nicol for the Roxburgh Club, 1844. Howard family.

FISKE, R.C. 'The Howards of Brockdish and Hackney', *N.Anc.* 1(3), 1978, 33-5. Pedigree, 15-18th c.

GRANT, NEIL. *The Howards of Norfolk.* Franklin Watts, 1972. Includes brief pedigree, 16-20th c.

HOWARD, CHARLES. *Historical anecdotes of some of the Howard family.* New ed. W. Clarke, 1817.

HOWARD, HENRY. *Indications of memorials, monuments, paintings, and engravings of persons of the Howard family and of their wives and children, and of those who have married ladies of the name, and of the representatives of some of its branches now extinct ...* 2 vols. Corby Castle: [ ], 1834-6.

M[ARSHALL], G.W. 'Genealogies of the surname of Howard', *East Anglian* 2, 1866, 341-2. Lists many early works on the Howards.

RICHARDSON, ETHEL M.E. *The lion and the rose (the great Howard story), Norfolk line 957-1646, Suffolk line 1603-1917.* 2 vols. Hutchinson, [1922].

ROBINSON, JOHN MARTIN. *The Dukes of Norfolk.* Oxford: Oxford U.P., 1983. Howard family; includes pedigrees, 14-20th c., with a select bibliography. Of Suffolk, Norfolk, Sussex and Derbyshire.

RYE, WALTER. 'Doubtful Norfolk pedigrees, no.1: Howard', *Genealogist* 2, 1878, 337-43. Medieval.

Howard *continued*

For other works on the Howards, see *Suffolk: a genealogical bibliography*, section 7.

Howlett

RYE, WALTER. 'The yeoman families of Norfolk: no.1: Howlett', *East Anglian* 2, 1865, 263-5. 14-18th c.

SHAW, M. 'The families: Howlett and White', *Norfolk fair* 3(10), 1971, 14-21.

Howman

H. C., & COOPER, THOMPSON. 'Roger Howman, M.D., Edward Howman, M.D., and others of the family', *East Anglian* 2, 1866, 99. 18-19th c.

'Genealogical memoranda relating to the Howman family', *M.G.H.* N.S. 1, 1874, 398-9. 16-17th c.

Hunter

See Master and Montgomerie

Hurry

HURRY-HOUGHTON, THOMAS, & MARGARET. *Memorials of the family of Hurry of Great Yarmouth, and of America, Australia and South Africa.* Liverpool: C. Tinling & Co., 1926. 18-20th c.

PALMER, CHARLES JOHN. *Memorials of the family of Hurry of Great Yarmouth, Norfolk, and of New York, United States.* Norwich: Miller and Leavins, 1873. 18-19th c.

Inglos

'Inglos of Loddon Inglos, Co.Norfolk', *M.G.H.* 5th series 9, 1935-7, 286-8. Pedigree, 11-16th c.

Ivory

EVANS, MARGARET CAREY. 'The descendants of Thomas Ivory', *N.A.* 38, 1986, 206-14. 18-19th c.

Jarrold

OLIVER, M. 'The families, 2: the Jarrolds', *Norfolk fair* 4(5), 1971, 30-38.

Jermy

JERMY, KENNETH E. 'Captain Seth Jermy R.N.', *N.Anc.* 4(7), 1987, 106-8. See also 4(8), 1987, 124-8. Includes pedigree of Jermy, 17-18th c.

VALDAR, STEWART. *A brief history of the Jermy family of Norfolk and Suffolk.* [New ed.] The author, 1976. Includes pedigree, 13-20th c.

Jermyn

RYE, WALTER. 'Pedigree of the family of Jermyn of Woodton in Norfolk and Halesworth in Suffolk', *Herald & genealogist* 5, 1870, 435-43. 17-19th c.

Julius

FYSH, J.P.G., & FYSH, A.V.G.A. 'A brief history of
the Julius family', *N.Anc.* **4**(4), 1986, 52-55.
Includes pedigree, 17-19th c.

Kemp

HITCHIN-KEMP, FRED, et al. *A general history of the
Kemp and Kempe families of Great Britain and
her colonies, with arms, pedigrees ... &c.*
Leadenhall Press, 1902-3. Also of Cornwall,
Dorset, Staffordshire, Suffolk, Hampshire, etc.
Includes many pedigrees.

Kenton

See Hammond

Kerslake

LONGSDON, E.H. *Kerslake of Norfolk, with Blythe
and Lanchester*. Portsmouth: Charpentier, 1937.
Includes folded pedigrees, 18-20th c.

Kett

KETT, L.M. *The Ketts of Norfolk: a yeoman family*.
Mitchell Hughes & Clarke, 1921.

Knightley

'Stemmata et propagationes antiquae familiae de
Knightley', *M.G.H.* N.S. **1**, 1868, 88-101. Of
Northamptonshire, Norfolk, Warwickshire, etc.,
shows connections with many other families,
medieval-17th c.

Knyvett

BLOOM, J. HARVEY. 'Proof of the parentage of
Alice Knyvet, died 1474', *Genealogists
magazine* **5**, 1931, 362-3.

BULEEP, SINGH F.V. 'The Knyvett family', *N.A.M.*
2nd series **3**, 1908, 80-7. Pedigree compiled
1651.

SCHOFIELD, BERTRAM, ed. *The Knyvett letters
1620-1644*. N.R.S. **20**, 1949. Includes pedigree
of Knyvett, 16-17th c.

VIRGOE, ROGER. 'The earlier Knyvetts: the rise of a
Norfolk gentry family', *N.A.* **41**, 1990, 1-14.
Includes pedigree, 14-16th c. Pt.1 only
published so far.

See also Gawdy

Lanchester

See Kerslake

Langham

See Hammond

Langley

WEST, ROSALIE. 'Matthew, Matthew, wherefore art
thou, Matthew?', *N.Anc.* **6**(1), 1990, 9-11.
Langley family; includes pedigree, 18-19th c.

Lavile

COZENS-HARDY, B. 'The Lavile and Curson
families of Letheringsett', *N.A.* **30**, 1952, 338-
52. Includes pedigree of Curson, 15-17th c.

Legge

LEGGE, A.G. 'Some account of the Legge family
resident in East Anglia', *N.A.* **13**, 1898, 101-15.
Medieval; of South Creake and Syderstone.
Includes abstracts of 16 deeds.

Le Neve

LE NEVE-FOSTER, PETER. *The Le Neves of Norfolk:
a family history*. Sudbury: the author, 1969.

RYE, FRANCIS. *Calendar of correspondence and
documents relating to the family of Oliver Le
Neve of Witchingham, Norfolk, 1675-1743*. ed.
Walter Rye. Norwich: A.H. Goose, 1895.

See also Gawdy

Lennard

BARRETT-LEONARD, SIR THOMAS. *An account of the
families of Lennard and Barrett compiled
largely from original documents*. Spottiswoode
& Co., 1908. Includes material on the Fynes and
Dacre families.

Le Strange

EWEN, C. L.'ESTRANGE. *Observations on the Le
Stranges, with some corrections of prevalent
genealogical errors*. Paignton: C.L. Ewen,
1946. Pamphlet. Of Norfolk, Shropshire and
Warwickshire. Includes pedigree, 13-15th c.

KETTON-CREMER, R.W. 'Sir Hamon L'Estrange and
his sons', in his *Norfolk gallery*. Faber & Faber,
1948, 56-94. 17th c.

LE STRANGE, HAMON. 'Calendar of Le Strange
papers selected from the muniment room at
Hunstanton Hall, Norfolk', in HISTORICAL
MANUSCRIPTS COMMISSION *The manuscripts of
the Duke of Leeds, the Bridgewater Trust,
Reading Corporation, the Inner Temple, &c.*
11th report, appendix, pt.7. C.5060-vii.
H.M.S.O., 1888, 93-118. Mainly Le Strange
family letters, 17-18th c.

LE STRANGE, HAMON. *Le Strange records: a
chronicle of the early Le Stranges of Norfolk
and the March of Wales A.D. 1100-1310, with
the lines of Knockin and Blackmere continued to
their extinction*. Longmans Green & Co., 1916.

Lenham

DUNLOP, J. RENTON. 'Pedigree of the Lenham
family of Norfolk, Kent, and Berkshire',
M.G.H. 5th series **6**, 1926-8, 281-7. 12-16th c.

Lincoln

LEA, J. HENRY, & HUTCHINSON, J.R. *The ancestry of Abraham Lincoln*. Boston: Houghton Mifflin, 1909. Norfolk family, 17-19th c., includes folded pedigree.

RYE, WALTER. 'Abraham Lincoln's probable Norfolk ancestors', in his *Some historical essays chiefly relating to Norfolk* 6. Norwich: H.W. Hunt, 1927, 257-77. 17-18th c.

STEER, FRANCIS W. 'Lincoln's ancestors and Swanton Morley', *Notes & queries* 186, 1944, 156-7. 17th c.

Lombard

See Walpole

Lovell

HARRISON, GEORGE LOVELL. 'A few notes on the Lovells of East Harling', *N.A.* 18, 1914, 46-77. 15-17th c.

Lubbock

BIRKBECK, ROBERT. *Notes on the history and genealogy of the family of Lubbock*. Mitchell & Hughes, 1891. Includes pedigree, 15-19th c.

Lumner

See Tirrel

Mackerell

B., C.J. 'Notes on the family of Mackerell of Norwich', *East Anglian* N.S. 13, 1909-10, 108-9 & 141-2. 17-18th c.

Mallett

MALLETT, B. 'Which was his father?', *N.Anc.* 4(3), 1986, 45-6. Mallett family pedigrees, 17-19th c.

Marshall

M[ARSHALL], G.W. 'Marshall of Barncaster, Co.Norfolk', *East Anglian* 4, 1871, 31-2. 18th c.

MARSHALL, G.W. 'Notes on the surname of Marshall in Norfolk', *East Anglian* 2, 1865, 143-6. Medieval.

Martineau

CROFTON, C. ANTHONY. *Pedigrees of the Martineau family: a revision and continuation of pedigrees set forth in 1907 by David Martineau in Notes on the pedigree of the Martineau family ...* Northampton: Archer & Goodman, 1972. Huguenot family; includes folded pedigrees.

TALLACK, T.R. 'French refugees in Norfolk', *East Anglian* N.S. 1, 1885-6, 33-5 & 53-5. See also 70. Martineau family.

Master

MASTER, ALFRed. *Genealogy of the family of Master of Henhurst, Kent and Norfolk; with the extinct family of Master of Willesborough, Co.Kent, and some notices of the allied families of Grimwood, Turner, Hunter, Torriano, and Hawtayne*. Norwich: Frederick Crowe, 1881.

Mileham

TENISON, C.M. 'Mileham of Buckingham, Norfolk', *M.G.H.* 3rd series 3, 1900, 202-4. 16-17th c.

See also Browne

Montgomerie

FRANKLYN, CHARLES A.H. *A genealogical history of the families of Montgomerie of Garboldisham, Hunter of Knapp, and Montgomerie of Fittleworth*. Ditchling: Ditchling Press, 1967. 14-20th c. Knapp, Perthshire; Fittleworth, Sussex.

Morley

RICHMOND, COLIN. 'Thomas Lord Morley (d.1416) and the Morleys of Hingham', *N.A.* 38, 1983, 1-12.

Moubray

See Albini

Moulton

See Warde

Muriel

MURIEL, J.H.L. *A Fenland family: some notes on the history of a family surnamed Muriel*. Ipswich: East Anglian magazine, 1968. Of Cambridgeshire, Norfolk and Suffolk; includes pedigrees, parish register extracts, monumental inscriptions, etc.

Nelson

JAMES, A. 'Hilborough church and the Nelsons', *East Anglian magazine* 26, 1967, 280-81. 18-19th c. Brief note.

MATCHAM, M. EYRE. *The Nelsons of Burnham Thorpe: a record of a Norfolk family compiled from unpublished letters and notebooks, 1787-1842*. John Lane, 1911.

NELSON, EDMUND. 'A family historicall register', *N.N.N.Q.* 1st series, 1896-9, 140-44. Nelson family—written in 1781.

NELSON, THOMAS. *A genealogical history of the Nelson family*. Rev. ed. Kings Lynn: Thew & Son, 1908. Includes pedigrees, 17-19th c., also pedigrees of associated families, monumental inscriptions, etc.

Norris

RYE, W. 'The families of Norris of Norfolk', *N.A.M.* 2nd series **1**, 1906, 48-51.

Norwich

GOWERS, W.R. 'The de Norwich family', *East Anglian* N.S. **3**, 1889-90, 259-61. Medieval.

Oxley

HOVENDEN, ROBERT. 'Oxley', *M.G.H.* 3rd series **2**, 1898, 74-6. Oxley family of Norfolk and London, etc., extracts from family bible, 18-19th c.

Page

GOWER, GRANVILLE LEVESON. 'Page family', *M.G.H.* 2nd series **5**, 1884, 279-80. Extracts from Saxthorpe parish register, 16-17th c., with some monumental inscriptions.

PAGE, RAYMOND A. 'The Page family in Norfolk: the Pages of Saxthorpe', *N.Anc.* **2**(6), 1981, 79-81. 15-18th c.

PAGE, RAYMOND A. 'The Page family in Norfolk', *N.Anc.* **2**(5), 1981, 65-7. Medieval.

PAGE, RAYMOND A. 'The Page family in Norfolk: the Page's of Walcot, Acle and Ormesby', *N.Anc.* **2**(11), 1982, 151-3. Includes pedigree, 16-17th c.

Palgrave

This family has been much researched. The major nineteenth-century work was:

PALMER, CHARLES JOHN, & TUCKER, STEPHEN. *Palgrave family memorials.* Norwich: Miller and Leavins, 1878. 16-18th c., includes pedigrees, parish register extracts, wills, etc.

Much further work has been completed in the 20th century; the main authority is now:

PALGRAVE, DEREK A., & PALGRAVE-MOORE, PATRICK T.R. *The history and lineage of the Palgraves.* Doncaster: Palgrave Society, 1978. Of Norfolk and Suffolk, 12-20th c. Includes many pedigrees and brief biographies.

Other works include:

PALGRAVE, DEREK A. *Archives at Flegg relating to the Palgraves.* Doncaster: Palgrave Society, 1975. Parish register extracts, will abstracts, census returns, etc., etc. 17-19th c.

PALGRAVE, DEREK A. *North Barningham: the church, the hall and the Palgrave family.* Doncaster: the author, 1974. Includes Palgrave pedigrees, 16-18th c.

PALGRAVE, DEREK A. *The Palgraves of Rollesby: a brief history, 1773-1973.* Doncaster: the author, 1973. Includes pedigrees.

Palgrave continued

PALGRAVE-MOORE, PATRICK T.R. *The Palgraves of Ludham.* Monograph 5. Doncaster: Palgrave Society, 1977. Includes pedigree, 18-20th c.

Reference may also be made to the Palgrave Society's newsletter:

Palgrave newsletter. Doncaster: Palgrave Society, 1974-82. Continued by: *Palgrave chronicle: the offial journal of the Palgrave Society.* Doncaster: the Society, 1983-. Includes a number of Palgrave pedigrees.

There are also a number of briefer articles:

MORIARTY, GEORGE ANDREWS. 'The parentage and ancestry of Dr. Richard Palgrave of Charlestown, Massachusetts', *New England historical and genealogical register* **102**, 1948, 87-98 & 312-3. Pagrave or Palgrave family, of Pagrave and Thruxton, Norfolk.

PALGRAVE, DEREK A. 'The rise and fall of North Barningham Hall', *N.Anc.* **1**(8), 1979, 103-5. Palgrave family, 15-18th c.

'Family of Pagrave or Palgrave', *East Anglian* **3**, 1869, 98-101. Pedigree, 16-17th c.

Parker

PARKER, A.J. 'The persistence of an uncommon Christian name', *N.Anc.* **1**(10), 1980, 132-33. Parker family, includes pedigree, 18-19th c.

Paston

The Pastons are today one of the most well-known families of fifteenth century England. This is due to the survival of their letters, which have been edited by many different hands. The most important editions are:

DAVIS, NORMAN, ed. *Paston letters and papers of the fifteenth century.* 2 vols. Oxford: Clarendon Press, 1976.

GAIRDNER, JAMES, ed. *The Paston letters.* New complete library ed. Chatto & Windus, 1904.

See also:

BUHLER, CURT F. 'Some new Paston documents', *Review of English Studies* **14**, 1938, 129-42. 15-16th c.

There have been many studies based on these letters; they include:

BARBER, RICHARD, ed. *The Pastons: a family in the Wars of the Roses.* Folio Society, 1981.

BENNETT, H.S. *The Pastons and their England: studies in an age of transition.* 2nd ed. Cambridge: C.U.P., 1932.

BRITNELL, R.H. 'The Pastons and their Norfolk', *Agricultural History review* **36**, 1988, 132-44. A study of 15th c. estate management.

Paston continued

RICHMOND, COLIN. 'The Pastons revisited: marriage and the family in fifteenth-century England', *Bulletin of the Institute of Historical Research* **58**, 1985, 25-36.

RICHMOND, COLIN. *The Paston family in the fifteenth century: the first phase.* Cambridge: Cambridge University Press, 1990. Includes pedigree.

ROWLING, MARJORIE A. 'New evidence on the disseisin of the Pastons from their Norfolk manor of Gresham, 1448-1451', *N.A.* **40**, 1989, 302-8.

TURNER, DAWSON, ed. *Sketch of the history of Caister Castle, near Yarmouth, including biographical notices of Sir John Fastolfe and of different individuals of the Paston family.* Whittaker & Co., 1842. Includes pedigree of Paston, 15-17th c.

VIRGOE, ROGER. *Paston letters: illustrated letters of the Paston family: private life in the fifteenth century.* Macmillan, 1989.

Two works dealing with the family in the 16-17th centuries are worth consulting:

WYNDHAM, KATHERINE S.H. 'An Elizabethan search: the Norfolk Pastons and the Tower archives', *Archives* **14**, 1980, 211-16. 15-16th c.

HUGHEY, RUTH, ed. *The correspondence of Lady Katherine Paston, 1603-1627.* N.R.S. **14**, 1941. Includes pedigree, 16-17th c., and biographical notes on the 'chief personages'.

A number of works deal with the family in the longer term:

BURSTALL, E.B. 'The Pastons and their manor of Binham', *N.A.* **30**, 1952, 101-29. Includes pedigree, 15-19th c., also of Clarke and England families, 18-19th c., with list of lords and stewards of Binham.

MARSHALL, K.N. *The Pastons, 1378-1732.* Norwich: Jarrold & Sons, [1956].

WORSHIP, FRANCIS. 'Account of a ms. genealogy of the Paston family in the possession of His Grace the Duke of Norfolk', *N.A.* **4**, 1855, 1-55. Includes folded pedigree, medieval-18th c.

The Pastons: the story of a Norfolk family. *Catalogue of loan exhibition at the Norwich Castle Museum.* Norwich: the Museum, 1953. 15-19th c.

Payne

CARTHEW, G.A. 'On the right of wardship and the ceremony of homage & fealty in the feudal times', *N.A.* **4**, 1855, 286-91. Concerns the Payne family, 15th c.

Pepys

PEPYS, WALTER COURTENAY. *Genealogy of the Pepys family, 1273-1887.* 2nd ed. Faber & Faber, 1951. Norfolk and Cambridgeshire. Includes pedigrees and wills.

Pitman

PITMAN, CHARLES E. *History and pedigree of the family of Pitman of Dunchideock, Exeter, and their collaterals, and of the Pitmans of Alphington, Norfolk, and Edinburgh, with part pedigrees and account of families connected by marriage ....* Mitchell Hughes & Clarke, 1920. Medieval-19th c.

Potts

See Tirrel

Pulvertaft

'Some Pulvertafts of Witchingham, Norfolk', *Pulvertaft papers* **3**(2), 1992, 10-11. 16th c.

'The Pulvertafts of Kings Lynn', *Pulvertaft papers* **3**(1), 1991, 2-7. Includes pedigree, 17-18th c.

Quarles

MARSHALL, GEORGE W. 'A genealogy of the Quarles family', *East Anglian* **3**, 1869, 155-9, 170-73, 184-7, 196-7, 203-7, 225, 227-31, 241-4, 282, 287 & 307-9; **4**, 1871, 137 & 255. Of Norfolk and Essex, 16-17th c.

Rainsford

BUCKLAND, EMILY A. *The Rainsford family with sidelights on Shakespeare, Southampton, Hall and Hart, embracing 1000 years of the Rainsford family ...* Worcester: Phillips and Probert, 1832. Of Essex, Norfolk, Suffolk, Oxfordshire, Gloucestershire, Worcestershire, Warwickshire, Northamptonshire and various other counties; includes pedigrees.

Ramsey

WHITTINGHAM, ARTHUR. 'The Ramsey family of Norwich', *Archaeological journal* **137**, 1980, 285-9. Medieval masons.

Raven

See Hardy

Reckitt

RECKITT, B.N. *The history of Reckitt and Sons, Ltd.* Norwich: A. Brown & Sons, 1951. History of a family business; includes pedigree, 17-20th c.

Rede

WHITE, HELENE P. 'Notes on the families of Rede and Symonds', *N.A.* **30**, 1952, 232-3. 16th c.

Reymes

RAIMES, ALWYN LESLIE. 'Reymes of Overstrand', *N.A.* **30**, 1952, 15-64. Includes pedigrees, 13-20th c., wills, parish register extracts, monumental inscriptions, deeds, etc.

Richardson

SAMBROOK, J.J. 'Honingham Hall, Norfolk', *N.A.* **34**, 1969, 303-13. Includes notes on the Richardson and Townshend families, 16-20th c.

Roberts

ROBERTS, SAMUEL, ET AL. *Some memorials of the Roberts of Queens Tower, Sheffield and Cockley Cley, Swaffham, Norfolk, as exemplified by kindred, affinity and marriage.* 4th ed. Sheffield: J.W. Northend, 1971. 16-20th c., includes folded pedigrees.

Rolfe

BERRY, VERONICA. *The Rolfe papers: the chronicle of a Norfolk family, 1559-1908.* Norwich: the author, 1979. A family history; includes pedigrees.

GUNTHER, A.E. *Rolfe family records.* 2 vols (described as vol.1 & 3). Heacham: privately printed, 1962. 19-20th c. Vol.2 was published as GUNTHER, R.T., & GUNTHER, A. *Rolfe family records, volume II.* Hazell, Watson & Viney, 1914, and is updated by vols.1 & 3.

Rye

RYE, WALTER. *An account of the family of Rye.* Mitchell & Hughes, 1876. Parts originally published in *Herald and genealogist* 6, 1871, 33-42; **7**, 1873, 235-49 & **8**, 1874, 401-14, and in *Genealogist* **1**, 1877, 67-80 & 122-6. Medieval-19th c.

RYE, WALTER. 'Rye of Hingham', *N.A.M.* **3**, 1887, 250. Includes folded pedigree, 11-16th c.

Sainty

SAINTY, J.C. 'Some speculations on the origin of the family of Sainty', *N.Anc.* **2**(3), 1980, 35-6. 17-18th c.

Say

HORTON-SMITH, L.G.H. 'Some Says of Norfolk', *Notes & queries* **193**, 1948, 516-7. Chancery case, 1663.

Sayer

MARSHALL, G.W. 'Extracts from the parish registers of Thurlton, Co.Norfolk, relating to the family of Sayer', *M.G.H.* N.S. **1**, 1874, 18. 18th c.

Scambler

BIRD, ALAN. 'Bishop Scambler's family', *N.Anc.* **1**(10), 1980, 127-30. 16-17th c.

Shakespeare

See Rainsford

Sheen

CAMPLING, ARTHUR. 'Sheen of Shotesham All Saints and Swainsthorpe, Co.Norfolk', *M.G.H.* 5th series **9**, 1935-7, 37-41. Pedigree, 14-19th c.

Shelly

SHELLY, JOHN. *Memorials of the family of Shelly of Great Yarmouth, their ancestors and descendants.* Phillimore & Co., 1909. Includes pedigree, 17-19th c.

Shelton

ARMSTRONG, B.J. 'Notes on the church and family of Shelton', *N.A.* **12**, 1895, 234-42. 15-16th c.

Sheppard

J., E.C. 'A family bible, 1744', *E.A.M.* **1922**, 7, 10, 11 & 13. Sheppard, Crickmer and Burton families of Norfolk and Suffolk.

Shorting

SHORTING, ERNEST H.H. 'Shorting family', *M.G.H.* 5th series **2**, 1917, 299-305. 16-20th c.

Shuldham

DASHWOOD, G.H. 'Notes on a pedigree of the time of Henry the Sixth, showing the title of Thomas Shuldham, esq., to the manor of Watlington', *N.A.* **6**, 1864, 300-303. 14-18th c.

Skottowe

SKOTTOWE, PHILLIP F. *The leaf and the tree: the story of an English family.* Research Publishing, 1963. Of Norfolk, Yorkshire and Buckinghamshire, etc., medieval-20th c.

Soame

MUSKETT, J.J. 'Soame family', *East Anglian* N.S. **3**, 1889-90, 328. Pedigree, 15-16th c.

Southampton

See Rainsford

Spelman

RYE, W. 'Spelman of Norfolk', *N.A.M.* 2nd series **1**, 1906, 71-8.

Spenser

RYE, WALTER. 'The possible East Anglian descent of the poet Spenser', *N.A.* **19**, 1917, 175-82. 16th c.

Stapelton

LEE-WARNER, JAMES. 'The Stapeltons of Ingham', *N.A.* **8**, 1879, 183-223. Includes pedigree, 13-15th c., will of Sir Miles Stapelton, 1466, etc.

Styleman

JAMES, ELIZABETH M. 'The Old Hall, Snettisham, and the Styleman family', *N.A.* **38**, 1983, 343-57. Includes pedigree, 17-19th c.

Surrey

See Warrene

Symonds

See Rede

Taylor

TAYLOR, PHILIP MEADOWS. *A memoir of the family of Taylor of Norwich.* Spottiswoode & Co., 1886. 18-19th c.

Tebbell

TEBBLE, NORMAN. 'The Tebbell-Tebble -Teble family of Stibbard', *N.Anc.* **4**(2), 1986, 21-3. 18-19th c.

Thaxter

RYE, W. 'The yeoman families of Norfolk, no.2: Thaxter of Bassingham', *East Anglian* **3**, 1866, 35-8. 16-18th c.

Theobald

LEIGHTON, H.R. 'Two East Anglian families in Durham: I: Theobalds of Rushall, Norfolk', *East Anglian* N.S. **11**, 1905-6, 322-4. 17-18th c.

Thurton

P[ARTRIDGE], C. 'Thurton family', *E.A.M.* **1930**, passim. 16-17th c.

Tindale

PRETYMAN, WILLIAM. 'Family of Tindale', *Genealogist* N.S. **26**, 1910, 16-24 & 82-93. Of Northamptonshire and Norfolk; medieval-17th c.

Tirrel

PURDY, R.J.W. 'Mannington Hall', *N.A.* **14**, 1901, 321-8. Includes pedigree of Tirrel, Lumner and Potts, 13-18th c.

Torriano

See Master

Townshend

DURHAM, JAMES. *The Townshends of Raynham, part 1: 1398-1600.* Cambridge: Deighton Bell & Co., 1922. No more published.

Townshend *continued*

HISTORICAL MANUSCRIPTS COMMISSION. *The manuscripts of the Marquess Townshend.* 11th report, appendix, pt.4. C.5060-iii. H.M.S.O., 1887. Includes many 18th c. letters of the Townshend family.

RYE, WALTER. 'Doubtful Norfolk pedigrees, II: Townshend', *Genealogist* **3**, 1879, 78-9. 14th c.

TOWNSHEND, CHARLES HERVEY. *The Townshend family of Lynn, in old and new England, genealogical and biographical.* 4th ed. New Haven, Conn: Tuttle, Morehouse & Taylor, 1884. Reprinted with additions from *New England historical and genealogical register* **29**, 1875.

'The duelling Townshends of Raynham', *N.Anc.* **1**(8), 1979, 99-102. Includes pedigree, 17-18th c.

See also Richardson

Tuddenham

VIRGOE, ROGER. 'The divorce of Sir Thomas Tuddenham', *N.A.* **34**, 1969, 406-18. 15th c.

Tufts

TUFTS, JAY FRANKLIN. *Tufts family history: a true account and history of our Tufts families, from and before 1638-1963.* Cleveland, Ohio: [ ], [1963].

Turner

TURNER, HARWARD. *The Turner family of Mulbarton and Great Yarmouth in Norfolk, 1547-1906: collections & notes.* New ed. by Frederick Johnson. Jarrold & Sons, 1907. Includes folded pedigrees.

Tuthill

See Dalyson

Tye

SUCKLING, F.H. 'Some notes on the parentage of Dionysia de Tye', *Genealogist* N.S. **25**, 1909, 78-82. 14th c.

Upwood

MANNING, C.R. 'Pedigree of Upwood, Terrington St.Clements, Co.Norfolk', *M.G.H.* 2nd series **4**, 1892, 248-52, 258-60 & 281-5. 16-18th c.

MANNING, C.R. *Pedigree of the family of Upwood, of Lovells Hall, Terrington St.Clement's, County Norfolk.* Privately printed, 1891.

Valoignes

TINGEY, J.C. 'The Barony of Valoignes in Norfolk', *N.A.* **22**, 1926, 292-310. Medieval.

Vincent

See Hooker

Wall

TRAPPES-LOMAX, T.B. 'The parentage and family of the martyr Blessed John Wall, O.F.M.', *Recusant history* **6**, 1961-2, 195-99. Includes 17th c. pedigree.

Walpole

BROOME, JOHN H. *Houghton and the Walpoles*. Kings Lynn: Simpkin Marshall & Co., 1865.

RYE, WALTER. 'Doubtful Norfolk pedigrees, no.III: Walpole', *Genealogist* **3**, 1879, 79-80. See also N.S. **22**, 1906, 207-8. 14th c.

WAGNER, HENRY. 'Peter Lombard of Nismes and his immediate descendants', *Genealogist* N.S. **35**, 1919, 52-5. 17-19th c., descendants include the Walpole family.

RYE, WALTER. 'Notes on the early pedigree of the family of Walpole of Houghton', *N.A.M.* **1**, 1877, 267-84. Medieval.

SUCKLING, F.H. 'Some notes on Dorothy Walpole and her descendants', *East Anglian* N.S. **10**, 1903-4, 347-51. See also N.S. **11**, 1905-6, 15-16. 17-18th c.

JESSOPP, AUGUSTUS. *One generation of a Norfolk house: a contribution to Elizabethan history*. 3rd ed. T. Fisher Unwin, 1913. Life of Henry Walpole, 1558-95, with some account of other members of his family.

RYE, WALTER. *The later history of the family of Walpole of Norfolk, to which is prefixed some remarks as to the probable identity of the Houghton family with the early merchants of Kings Lynn*. Norwich: H.W. Hunt, 1920.

VADE-WALPOLE, H.S. 'Notes on the Walpoles, with some account of a junior branch', *Genealogical magazine* **2**, 1899, 235-48, 300-306, 364-71, 390-96, 433-8, 490-94 & 550-52; **3**, 1900, 1-13. 17-19th c.

WALPOLE, NANCY. *The Walpoles of Wolterton*. Lewes: Book Guild, 1986.

Warde

JONES, W.H. 'The English background of some early settlers of Hampton, New Hampshire, from Ormesby St.Margaret', *New England historical and genealogical register* **141**, 1987, 114-27 & 313-29. Notes on the Warde, Goodwin and Moulton families.

Warrene

COAD, J.G., & STREETON, A.D.F. 'Excavations at Castle Acre Castle, Norfolk, 1972-77: county house and castle of the Norman Earls of Surrey', *Archaeological journal* **139**, 1982, 138-301. Includes notes on the Warrene family, Earls of Surrey.

White

TAYLOR, RICHARD J. 'Dear old John White', *N.Anc.* **4**(6), 1987, 90-92. Includes White pedigree, 18-19th c.

GODFREY, JOHN T., & WARD, JAMES. *The homes and haunts of Henry Kirk White, with some account of the family of White of Nottingham and Norfolk*. Simpkin Marshall & Co., 1908. Includes folded pedigree, 18-19th c.

See also Howlett

Wiggon

'Family registers in a bible, psalm and prayer book, 1633', *M.G.H.* N.S. **2**, 1877, 587-8. Wiggon and Burrowes families.

Windesore

See Duckett

Windham

HEWLETT, W.O. 'The manuscripts of R.W. Ketton, esq., of Felbrigg Hall, Norfolk', in HISTORICAL MANUSCRIPTS COMMISSION *The manuscripts of the Duke of Beaufort, K.G., the Earl of Donoughmore, and others*. 12th report, appendix, pt.9. C.6338-i. H.M.S.O., 1891, 179-226. Windham family letters, 17-18th c.

KETTON-CREMER, R.W. *Felbrigg: the story of a house*. Rupert Hart-Davis, 1962. Wyndham family history, 16-19th c., includes pedigree.

KETTON-CREMER, R.W. 'Thomas Windham of Felbrigg', *N.A.* **27**, 1941, 417-28. Includes pedigree, 16th c., and monumental inscription.

SIMPSON, R.J. 'Extracts from the Felbrigg register relating to the Wyndham family and those connected with them', *M.G.H.* 2nd series **5**, 1894, 332-4. 18-19th c.

WYNDHAM, H.A. *A family history, 1410-1688: the Wyndhams of Norfolk and Somerset*. Oxford U.P., 1939.

Wodehouse

KIMBERLEY, JOHN, EARL OF *The Wodehouses of Kimberley*. Chiswick Press, 1887.

RYE, W. 'The Wodehouses of Kimberley and Waxham', *N.A.M.* 2nd series **1**, 1906, 143-61.

RYE, WALTER. 'Doubtful Norfolk pedigrees, no.IV: Wodehouse', *Genealogist* **3**, 1879, 129-32. 13-14th c.

Womack

CAMPLING, ARTHUR. 'Womack of Mautby, Co.Norfolk', *M.G.H.* 5th series **8**, 1932-4, 317-20. Pedigree, 16-19th c.

Wyer

WYER, PAT. 'Weavers and windmills', *N.Anc.* **3**(3), 1983, 30-33. Wyer family; includes pedigree, 16-19th c.

Wyndham

See Windham

Yallop

HOLLEYMAN, GEORGE A. *A history of the Yallop family, 1767-1986: an account of the descendants of James Yallop born in Great Yarmouth in the year 1767: to which is appended a list of inhabitants of that surname in the county of Norfolk dating back to the year 1505.* Henfield: [the author], 1987.

Young

THOMPSON, T.W. 'Youngs, Gibsons and their associates: an inquiry into the origin of certain East Anglian and metropolitan gypsy families', *Gypsy Lore Society journal* **24**, 1945, 44-56; **25**, 1946, 39-45. Norfolk, Suffolk and Essex.

8. PARISH REGISTERS AND OTHER RECORDS OF BIRTHS, MARRIAGES AND DEATHS

Parish registers are vital documents for the genealogist, and are frequently the first source consulted. A comprehensive study of original parish registers for Norfolk, with a full listing, is provided by:

PALGRAVE-MOORE, PATRICK T.R. *National index of parish registers vol.7: East Anglia: Cambridgeshire, Norfolk and Suffolk* Society of Genealogists, 1983.

See also:

NORFOLK RECORD OFFICE. *Parish registers deposited at the Norfolk Record Office.* Norwich: the Office, 1980.

These volumes do not, however, provide full listings of published parish registers. Norfolk is fortunate in having numerous published registers: many marriage registers were published at the turn of the last century in *Phillimore's parish register series*; more recently, the Norfolk and Norwich Genealogical Society has commenced its *The parish registers of Norfolk: monograph series* and its *Norfolk nonconformist registers: monograph series* (from 1983). A number of registers have also been privately published, and many extracts (sometimes fairly brief) have been printed in journals such as the *East Anglian*. All of these publications are listed below. This list must, however, be accompanied by a warning. Printed registers are copies, and copies can be mis-copied. Some transcribers of parish registers are very accurate; others, however, can make woeful errors. If possible, it is always best to check what is printed against the original manuscript. Before listing parish registers, a number of more general works concerned with births, marriages and deaths must be mentioned. For bishop's transcripts of parish registers, see:

BELL, SHEILA. *Index to bishop's transcripts from the Diocese of Norwich, 1685-1691.* N.N.G.S., 1986. Further volumes cover 1705 and 1715.

Marriage licences are a potentially important source; for Norfolk, however, only a brief time span is covered by:

HOOD, CHRISTINE, ed. *Norwich Archdeaconry marriage licence bonds, 1813-1837 (held at the Norfolk Record Office).* Norfolk genealogy **23**, 1991.

A longer time span—but a much smaller area—is covered by:

HAMLIN, P.E. 'Norfolk peculiar jurisdictions: index to marriage licence bonds, 1624-1860'. *Norfolk genealogy* **16**, 1984, 67-162.

Announcements of marriages and deaths printed in contemporary newspapers have been collected together and reprinted in:

SIMONS, JANICE. *Marriage and obituary notices, 1848. (Lynn Advertiser, Norfolk). Extracted from The Lynn Advertiser & West Norfolk Herald.* Kings Lynn: Janice Simons, 1992. Similar volumes are available covering 1880, 1881, 1882, 1890 and 1900; titles vary.

See also:

'Records of Fenland marriages', *F.N.Q.* **1**, 1889-91, 60-64. From old newspapers, covering Lincolnshire, Cambridgeshire, Norfolk and Huntingdonshire.

Many 'Norfolk strays', that is, notices of marriages and deaths of Norfolk people in other counties, are printed in most issues of the *Norfolk ancestor*; for example:

'Stray Norfolk marriages in vol.IV of *Suffolk parish registers* (Phillimores)', *N.Anc.* **1**(7), 1979, 97.

'Norfolk strays in Huntingdonshire', *N.Anc.* **2**(11), 1982, 154.

'Stray' marriages in Stepney are listed in:

BULLEN, R. FREEMAN. 'East Anglian marriages in Stepney registers', *E.A.M.* **1911**, 76, 78-9, 81-2, 83, 85-6, 89-90, 91, 98, 100-101, 103, 106, 108-9, 112, 117-8, 120-21, 123-4, 126-7 & 129-30; **1912**, 2-3, 5, 7-8, 10-11 & 13. Strays from Norfolk, Suffolk, Essex and Cambridgeshire, 1581-1719.

The following parish registers have been published; this list does not, however, include the many unpublished transcripts which have been made.

Acle

JOHNSON, F., ed. 'Marriages at Acle, 1664 to 1812', in PHILLIMORE, W.P.W., & JOHNSON, FREDERIC. *N.P.R.M.* **1**, *P.P.R.S.* **9**. Phillimore, 1899, 1-20.

Aldborough

JONES, HONOR. 'Index to Aldborough marriages, 1747-1811, Norfolk', *N.Anc.* **3**(7), 1984, 103.

Anmer

FARROW, M.A., ed. 'Marriages at Anmer, 1600 to 1837', in BLAGG, THOMAS M., & FARROW, MARGARET A., eds. *N.P.R.M.* **12**, *P.P.R.S.* **237**. Phillimore, 1936, 1-8.

Ashby

See Thurne

Ashwicken

DAUBENEY, A.R. VAUGHAN, ed. 'Marriages at Ashwicken with Leziate, 1717 to 1837', in his *N.P.R.M.* **10**, *P.P.R.S.* **225**. Phillimore, 1916, 99-104.

Attleborough

SANDERSON, E.W., ed. *Attleborough parish registers, 1552-1840.* Norfolk genealogy **12**, 1980.

Babingley

BLOOM, J. HARVEY, ed. 'Marriages at Babingly, 1662 to 1812', in PHILLIMORE, W.P.W., JOHNSON, FREDERIC, & BLOOM, J. HARVEY, eds. *N.P.R.M.* **2**, *P.P.R.S.* **13**. Phillimore, 1900, 129-30.

Bagthorp

FARROW, M.A., ed. 'Marriages at Bagthorpe, 1562 to 1837', in BLAGG, THOMAS M., & FARROW, MARGARET A., eds. *N.P.R.M.* **12**, *P.P.R.S.* **237**. Phillimore, 1936, 153-8.

Barton Bendish

FARROW, C.W., ed. *Barton Bendish All Ss. w. St.Mary, 1691-1837.* P.R.N. **14**, 1986.

FARROW, C.W., ed. *Barton Bendish St.Andrew, 1691-1837.* P.R.N. **15**, 1986.

Barton Turf

POOLE, J.G., ed. 'Marriages at Barton Turf, 1558 to 1837', in PHILLIMORE, W.P.W., & JOHNSON, FREDERIC, eds. *N.P.R.M.* **4**, *P.P.R.S.* **95**. Phillimore, 1909, 1-16.

Bawsey

BLOOM, J. HARVEY, ed. 'Marriages at Bawsey, 1539 to 1771', in PHILLIMORE, W.P.W., JOHNSON, FREDERICK, & BLOOM, J. HARVEY, eds. *N.P.R.M.* **2**, *P.P.R.S.* **13**. Phillimore, 1900, 1-4. See also *N.P.R.M.* **10**, *P.P.R.S.* **225**, 1916, 179-82.

Bedingham

TAYLOR, R. FETZER, ed. 'Marriages at Bedingham, 1561 to 1812', in PHILLIMORE, W.P.W., & JOHNSON, FREDERIC, eds. *N.P.R.M.* **4**, *P.P.R.S.* **95**. Phillimore, 1909, 133-47.

'Extracts from parish registers, no.36— Bedingham, Norfolk', *East Anglian* **4**, 1871, 270-75.

Bexwell

FARROW, C.W., ed. *Bexwell, 1558-1837.* P.R.N. **17**, 1987. Includes monumental inscriptions.

Billockby
HOLLEY, G.H., ed. 'Marriages at Billockby, 1561 to 1748', in PHILLIMORE, W.P.W., & HOLLEY, G.H., eds. *N.P.R.M.* **7**, *P.P.R.S.* **179**. Phillimore, 1912, 97-100.

Bircham Newton
HOWLETT, RICHARD, ed. *The parish register of Bircham Newton, from 1562 to 1743*. Norwich: A.H. Goose, 1888.

FARROW, M.A., ed. 'Marriages at Bircham Newton, 1562 to 1837', in BLAGG, THOMAS M., & FARROW, MARGARET A., eds. *N.P.R.M.* **12**, *P.P.R.S.* **237**. Phillimore, 1936, 141-6.

Bircham St.Mary
See Great Bircham

Bircham Tofts
FARROW, M.A., ed. 'Marriages at Bircham Tofts, or Bircham St.Andrew, 1698 to 1837', in BLAGG, THOMAS M., & FARROW, MARGARET A., eds. *N.P.R.M.* **12**, *P.P.R.S.* **23**. Phillimore, 1936, 147-51.

Bixley
M., C.R. 'Extracts from registers: Bixley, Norfolk', *East Anglian* N.S. **1**, 1885-6, 22-4. Brief.

Bodney
FARROW, C.W., & PALGRAVE-MOORE, PATRICK, eds. *Bodney, 1653-1837*. P.R.N. **2**, 1984. Includes monumental inscriptions.

Booton
ELWIN, W., ed. 'Marriages at Booton, 1560 to 1812', in PHILLIMORE, W.P.W., & JOHNSON, FREDERIC, eds. *N.P.R.M.* **3**, *P.P.R.S.* **75**. Phillimore, 1907, 71-83.

Boughton
FARROW, CHARLES W., ed. *Boughton, 1691-1837*. P.R.N. **12**, 1986.

Brampton
MICHELL, ARTHUR T. *The register of Brampton, Norfolk from 1732 to 1812, with all register bills extant from 1600 to 1732*. Sheriffhales: [ ], 1897.

Braydeston
JOHNSON, FRED, ed. 'Marriages at Braydeston, 1623 to 1812', in PHILLIMORE, W.P.W., & JOHNSON, FREDERIC, eds. *N.P.R.M.* **1**, *P.P.R.S.* **9**. Phillimore, 1899, 73-6.

Brundall
JOHNSON, F., ed. 'Marriages at +Brundall, 1563 to 1812', in PHILLIMORE, W.P.W., & JOHNSON, FREDERIC, eds. *N.P.R.M.* **1**, *P.P.R.S.* **9**. Phillimore, 1899, 31-5.

'Extracts from parish registers: Brundall, Norfolk', *East Anglian* **2**, 1866, 188-90. Brief.

Burgh
YATES, E.T. 'A transcript of the register of the parish of Burgh', *N.A.* **9**, 1884, 37-58. 1563-1810; includes list of incumbents, 16-19th c.

Burgh St.Margaret
HOLLEY, G.H., ed. 'Marriages at Burgh St.Margaret (Flegg Burgh), 1813 to 1837', in PHILLIMORE, W.P.W., & HOLLEY, G.H., eds. *N.P.R.M.* **7**, *P.P.R.S.* **179**. Phillimore, 1912, 93-5.

Burgh St.Peter
'Extracts from parish registers, 3: Bourrow St.Peter', *East Anglian* **1**, 1864, 268. Burgh St.Peter; brief extract.

Burlingham St.Andrew
JOHNSON, F., ed. 'Marriages at Burlingham St.Andrew, 1540 to 1812', in PHILLIMORE, W.P.W., & JOHNSON, FREDERIC, eds. *N.P.R.M.* **1**, *P.P.R.S.* **9**. Phillimore, 1899, 43-9.

Burlingham St.Peter
JOHNSON, F., ed. 'Marriages at Burlingham St.Peter, 1560 to 1812', in PHILLIMORE, W.P.W., & JOHNSON, FREDERIC, eds. *N.P.R.M.* **1**, *P.P.R.S.* **9**. Phillimore, 1899, 37-42.

Burnham Sutton
KINASTON, EDMUND, ed. 'Marriages at Burnham Sutton with Ulph, 1653 to 1837', in PHILLIMORE, W.P.W., & JOHNSON, FREDERIC, eds. *N.P.R.M.* **4**, *P.P.R.S.* **95**. Phillimore, 1909, 99-107.

Burnham Ulph
See Burnham Sutton

Caister next Yarmouth
HOLLEY, G.H., ed. 'Marriages at Caister-on-Sea, 1563 to 1837', in PHILLIMORE, W.P.W., & HOLLEY, G.H., eds. *N.P.R.M.* **7**, *P.P.R.S.* **179**. Phillimore, 1912, 1-40.

Calthorpe
JOHNSON, FRED, ed. 'Marriages at Calthorpe, 1558 to 1812', in PHILLIMORE, W.P.W., & JOHNSON, FREDERIC, eds. *N.P.R.M.* **1**, *P.P.R.S.* **9**. Phillimore, 1899, 89-96.

Carleton Rode

BENSLY, W.T., & BACK, A.J., eds. 'Marriages at Carleton Rode, 1560 to 1812', in PHILLIMORE, W.P.W., & JOHNSON, FREDERIC, eds. *N.P.R.M.* **4**, *P.P.R.S.* **95**. Phillimore, 1909, 67-97.

Castle Acre

JOHNSON, F., ed. 'Marriages at Castleacre, 1600 to 1707', in PHILLIMORE, W.P.W., & HOLLEY, G.H., eds. *N.P.R.M.* **5**, *P.P.R.S.* **148**. Phillimore, 1910, 151-2.

BLOOM, J. HARVEY, ed. 'Marriages at Castleacre, 1710 to 1812', in PHILLIMORE, W.P.W., & JOHNSON, FREDERIC, eds. *N.P.R.M.* **1**, *P.P.R.S.* **9**. Phillimore, 1899, 121-31.

Castle Rising

LEWIS, R.W.M., ed. 'Marriages at Castle Rising, 1573 to 1837', in his *N.P.R.M.* **9**, *P.P.R.S.* **215**. Phillimore, 1914, 83-98.

Chedgrave

JOHNSON, FRED., ed. 'Marriages at Chedgrave, 1550 to 1812', in PHILLIMORE, W.P.W., JOHNSON, FREDERIC, & BLOOM, J. HARVEY., eds. *N.P.R.M.* **2**, *P.P.R.S.* **13**. Phillimore, 1900, 131-57.

Cockley Cley

BANKOWSKY, HEATHER, ed. *Cockley Cley 1691-1837, with census returns 1841-1861*. P.R.N. **13**, 1986.

Colveston

See Didlington

Colney

PALGRAVE-MOORE, PATRICK, ed. *Colney 1705/6-1837*. P.R.N. **24**, 1987.

Congham

JOHNSON, FRED, & KERSLEY, S.R., eds. 'Marriages at Congham, 1581 to 1837', in LEWIS, R.W.M., ed. *N.P.R.M.* **9**, *P.P.R.S.* **215**. Phillimore, 1914, 37-55.

Costessy

SMITH, JOHN PETER, ed. 'Catholic registers of Costessey or Cossey Hall, Norfolk, the seat of the Jerningham family, Baronets, 1785-1821', *Publications of the Catholic Record Society* **22**, 1921, 276-303.

Cranwich

FARROW, CHARLES W., ed. *Cranwich, 1691-1837*. P.R.N. **10**, 1986.

Cringleford

COGSWELL, THOMAS S., ed. 'Marriages at Cringleford, 1561 to 1837', in PHILLIMORE, W.P.W., & HOLLEY, G.H., eds. *N.P.R.M.* **5**, *P.P.R.S.* **148**. Phillimore, 1910, 61-9.

Deopham

'Extracts from the parish registers of Deopham', *Genealogist* N.S. **10**, 1894, 256. 1569-1639.

Dereham

See Mattishall

Dersingham

LEWIS, R.W.M., ed. 'Marriages at Dersingham, 1653 to 1837', in BLAGG, THOMAS M., & FARROW, MARGARET A., eds. *N.P.R.M.* **12**, *P.P.R.S.* **237**. Phillimore, 1936, 9-38.

Dickleburgh

'Extracts from parish registers, no.33: Dickleburgh, Norfolk', *East Anglian* **4**, 1871, 181-2. Brief.

Didlington

FARROW, CHARLES W., ed. *Didlington with Colveston, 1691-1837*. P.R.N. **9**, 1986.

Diss

FARROW, CHARLES W., ed. *The parish registers of Diss, 1551-1837*. Norfolk genealogy **19**, 1987.

BODLE, A.N., ed. *Diss Particular Baptist Chapel: births 1806-1836*. N.N.R. **5**, 1987.

Ditchingham

TAYLOR, R. FETZER, ed. 'Marriages at Ditchingham, 1559 to 1812, in PHILLIMORE, W.P.W., & HOLLEY, G.H., eds. *N.P.R.M.* **5**, *P.P.R.S.* **148**. Phillimore, 1910, 81-103.

Docking

FARROW, M.A., ed. 'Marriages at Docking, with Southmere, 1558 to 1837', in BLAGG, THOMAS M., & FARROW, MARGARET A., eds. *N.P.R.M.* **12**, *P.P.R.S.* **237**. Phillimore, 1936, 75-107.

Downham Market

BODLE, A.N., ed. *Downham Market Wesleyan Methodist births and baptisms, 1814-1837*. N.N.R. **3**, 1986.

Dunham Magna

See Great Dunham

Dunston

PALGRAVE-MOORE, PATRICK. *Dunston, 1557-1837*. P.R.N. **3**, 1984.

Parish Registers, etc. continued

Dunton cum Doughton
ASTLEY, DR., ed. 'Marriages at Dunton-cum-Doughton, 1784 to 1837', in ASTLEY, H.J. DUKINFIELD, ed. *N.P.R.M.* **8**, *P.P.R.S.* **202**. Phillimore, 1914, 113-4.

Earlham
PALGRAVE-MOORE, PATRICK, ed. *Earlham, 1621-1837*. P.R.N. **29**, 1989.

East Barsham
MARTIN, W., & JOHNSON, F., eds. 'Marriages at East Barsham, 1658 to 1837', in PHILLIMORE, W.P.W., & BLAGG, THOS. M., eds. *N.P.R.M.* **6**, *P.P.R.S.* **157**. Phillimore, 1912, 61-9.

East Dereham
CARTHEW, G.A. *History of East Dereham.* Whittaker & Co., 1857. Includes parish register extracts, with several wills.
HARRISON, MABEL THELWALL. 'A glance at the parochial records, with some reminiscences of East Dereham', *East Anglian* N.S. **11**, 1905-6, 81-4 & 97-100. Parish register extracts, wills, etc.

East Lexham
BLOOM, J. HARVEY, ed. 'Marriages at East Lexham, 1541 to 1812', in PHILLIMORE, W.P.W., & JOHNSON, FREDERIC, eds. *N.P.R.M.* **1**, *P.P.R.S.* **9**. Phillimore, 1899, 113-20.

East Rainham
BLAGG, T.M., & ASTLEY, DUKINFIELD, eds. 'Marriages at East Rainham, 1601 to 1837', in DAUBENEY, A.R. VAUGHAN, ed. *N.P.R.M.* **11**, *P.P.R.S.* **232**. Phillimore, 1926, 125-42.

East Rudham
BLAGG, T.M., ed. 'Marriages at East Rudham, 1562 to 1837', in ASTLEY, H.J. DUKINFIELD, ed. *N.P.R.M.* **8**, *P.P.R.S.* **202**. Phillimore, 1914, 1-19.

East Somerton
See Winterton

East Walton
DAUBENEY, A.R.V., ed. 'Marriages at East Walton, 1560 to 1837', in his *N.P.R.M.* **10**, *P.P.R.S.* **225**. Phillimore, 1916, 51-64.

East Winch
DAUBENEY, A.R. VAUGHAN, ed. 'Marriages at East Winch, 1690 to 1838', in his *N.P.R.M.* **10**, *P.P.R.S.* **225**. Phillimore, 1916, 87-97.

Fakenham
GWYN, CECIL. 'Marriages at Fakenham, 1719 to 1837', in PHILLIMORE, W.P.W., & BLAGG, THOS. M., eds. *N.P.R.M.* **6**, *P.P.R.S.* **157**. Phillimore, 1912, 1-42.

Filby
HOLLEY, G.H., ed. 'Marriages at Filby, 1561 to 1837', in PHILLIMORE, W.P.W., & HOLLEY, G.H., eds. *N.P.R.M.* **7**, *P.P.R.S.* **179**. Phillimore, 1912, 71-92.

Flegg Burgh
See Burgh St.Margaret

Flitcham
STEPHENS, E.C., ed. 'Marriages at Flitcham, 1755 to 1837', in LEWIS, R.W.M., ed. *N.P.R.M.* **9**, *P.P.R.S.* **215**. Phillimore, 1914, 57-63.

Fordham
FARROW, CHARLES W., ed. *Fordham, 1576-1837.* P.R.N. **11**, 1986.

Foulden
PEARSON, WM. 'Extracts from parish registers: Foulden, Co.Norfolk', *East Anglian* N.S. **5**, 1893-4, 93.

Framingham Pigot
PEARSALL, M.E.R., ed. *Framingham Pigot Particular Baptist register: births, 1808-1836.* N.N.R. **2**, 1986.

Frenze
FARROW, C.W., ed. *Frenze: baptisms, 1654-1852; marriages, 1662-1852; burials, 1651-1877.* P.R.N. **6**, 1985.

Fring
HOLLEY, G.H., ed. 'Marriages at Fring, 1700 to 1812', in PHILLIMORE, W.P.W., & HOLLEY, G.H., eds. *N.P.R.M.* **5**, *P.P.R.S.* **148**. Phillimore, 1910, 77-80.

Gayton
DAUBENEY, A.R.V., ed. 'Marriages at Gayton, 1702 to 1837', in his *N.P.R.M.* **10**, *P.P.R.S.* **225**. Phillimore, 1916, 1-15.

Gayton Thorpe
DAUBENEY, A.R.V., ed. 'Marriages at Gayton Thorpe, 1575 to 1837', in his *N.P.R.M.* **10**, *P.P.R.S.* **225**. Phillimore, 1916, 17-32.

Gaywood
LEWIS, R.W.M., ed. 'Marriages at Gaywood, 1653 to 1837', in his *N.P.R.M.* **9**, *P.P.R.S.* **215**. Phillimore, 1914, 127-46.

Gooderstone

FARROW, C.W., ed. *Gooderstone, 1563-1837*. P.R.N. **23**, 1987.

Great Bircham

FARROW, M.A., ed. 'Marriages at Bircham St.Mary, or Great Bircham, 1669 to 1837', in BLAGG, THOMAS M., & FARROW, MARGARET A., eds. *N.P.R.M.* **12**, *P.P.R.S.* **237**. Phillimore, 1936, 129-39.

Great Cressingham

HESELTINE, ERNEST, ed. 'Marriages at Great Cressingham, 1557 to 1812', in PHILLIMORE, W.P.W., & JOHNSON, FREDERIC, eds. *N.P.R.M.* **3**, *P.P.R.S.* **75**. Phillimore, 1907, 117-33.

Great Dunham

BLOOM, J. HARVEY, ed. 'Marriages at Dunham Magna, 1538 to 1812', in PHILLIMORE, W.P.W., JOHNSON, FREDERIC, & BLOOM, J. HARVEY, eds. *N.P.R.M.* **2**, *P.P.R.S.* **13**. Phillimore, 1900, 11-32.

Great Massingham

DAUBENEY, A.R.V., ed. 'Marriages at Great Massingham, 1564 to 1837', in his *N.P.R.M.* **10**, *P.P.R.S.* **225**. Phillimore, 1916, 139-77.

Great Snoring

JOHNSON, FRED, ed. 'Marriages at Snoring Magna, 1560 to 1837', in PHILLIMORE, W.P.W., & BLAGG, THOS. M., eds. *N.R.P.M.* **6**, *P.P.R.S.* **157**. Phillimore, 1912, 87-106.

Great Yarmouth

BROWN, A. STUART, ed. 'Baptisms and deaths recorded in the Great Yarmouth Independent church book, 1643-1705, and biographical notes', *N.R.S.* **22**, 1951, 9-39.

Gresham

JERVIS, E.C., ed. 'Marriages at Gresham, 1690 to 1812', in PHILLIMORE, W.P.W., & JOHNSON, FREDERIC, eds. *N.P.R.M.* **4**, *P.P.R.S.* **95**. Phillimore, 1909, 149-54.

Grimstone

BLAGG, THOMAS M., & ELLABY, A.H., eds. 'Marriages at Grimston, 1552 to 1837', in LEWIS, R.W.M., ed. *N.P.R.M.* **9**, *P.P.R.S.* **215**. Phillimore, 1914, 1-35.

Hapton

GOLDSMITH, WENDY, ed. *Hapton Unitarian: births, baptisms and burials, 1792-1834. N.N.R.* **8**, 1989.

Hardwick

P., G.R. 'Surnames in parish registers: Hardwick, Norfolk', *East Anglian* **3**, 1869, 101-3. List, 1561-1800.

See also North Runcton

Harleston

See Redenhall

Haveringland

ROWLES, STEWART, ed. *Haveringland, 1694-1837, with Archdeacon's transcripts, 1600-1754*. P.R.N. **27**, 1989. Includes lists of vicars and monumental inscriptions.

Heacham

BLOOM, J. HARVEY, ed. 'Marriages at Heacham, 1558 to 1812', in PHILLIMORE, W.P.W., JOHNSON, FREDERIC, & BLOOM, J. HARVEY, eds. *N.P.R.M.* **2**, *P.P.R.S.* **13**. Phillimore, 1900, 77-98.

Hedenham

TAYLOR, R. FETZER, ed. 'Marriages at Hedenham, 1559 to 1812', in PHILLIMORE, W.P.W., & JOHNSON, FREDERIC, eds. *N.P.R.M.* **4**, *P.P.R.S.* **95**. Phillimore, 1909, 17-37.

Helhoughton

BLAGG, T.M., ET AL., eds. 'Marriages at Helhoughton, 1539 to 1837', in ASTLEY, H.J. DUKINFIELD, ed. *N.P.R.M.* **8**, *P.P.R.S.* **202**. Phillimore, 1914, 43-55.

Hemblington

JOHNSON, F., ed. 'Marriages at Hemblington, 1564 to 1812', in PHILLIMORE, W.P.W., & JOHNSON, FREDERIC, eds. *N.P.R.M.* **1**, *P.P.R.S.* **9**. Phillimore, 1899, 21-9.

Hemsby

'Marriages at Hemsby, 1556 to 1837', in PHILLIMORE, W.P.W., & HOLLEY, G.H., eds. *N.P.R.M.* **7**, *P.P.R.S.* **179**. Phillimore, 1912, 101-18.

Herringsby

See Stokesby

Hickling

JOHNSON, FREDERIC, ed. 'Marriages at Hickling, 1657 to 1812', in PHILLIMORE, W.P.W., & JOHNSON, FREDERIC, eds. *N.P.R.M.* **4**, *P.P.R.S.* **95**. Phillimore, 1909, 109-31.

Hillington

LEWIS, R.W.M., ed. 'Marriages at Hillington, 1695 to 1837', in his *N.P.R.M.* **9**, *P.P.R.S.* **215**. Phillimore, 1914, 65-75.

Holkham

BLOOM, J. HARVEY, ed. 'Marriages at Holkham, 1542 to 1812', in PHILLIMORE, W.P.W., JOHNSON, FREDERIC, & BLOOM, J. HARVEY, eds. *N.P.R.M.* **2**, *P.P.R.S.* **13**. Phillimore, 1900, 53-75.

Holme Hale

STALLARD, LEONARD B., ed. 'Marriages at Holme Hale, 1539 to 1837', in PHILLIMORE, W.P.W., & HOLLEY, G.H., eds. *N.P.R.M.* **5**, *P.P.R.S.* **148**. Phillimore, 1910, 21-36.

Holme Next Sea

JOHNSON, FREDK., ed. 'Marriages at Holme by the Sea', in PHILLIMORE, W.P.W., & HOLLEY, G.H., eds. *N.P.R.M.* **5**, *P.P.R.S.* **148**. Phillimore, 1910, 15-19.

Horningtoft

WILLIAMS, J.F., & SEAGRIM, C.P.C., eds. 'Marriages at Horningtoft, 1539 to 1837', in ASTLEY, H.J. DUKINFIELD, ed. *N.P.R.M.* **8**, *P.P.R.S.* **202**. Phillimore, 1914, 115-27.

Horstead

GLENCROSS, REGINALD M., ed. 'Marriages at Horstead, 1558 to 1812', in PHILLIMORE, W.P.W., & JOHNSON, FREDERIC, eds. *N.P.R.M.* **3**, *P.P.R.S.* **75**. Phillimore, 1907, 53-70.

Ickburgh

FARROW, C.W., ed. *Ickburgh, 1693-1837.* P.R.N. **19**, 1987.

Ingoldesthorpe

LEWIS, R.W.M., ed. 'Marriages at Ingoldisthorpe, 1754 to 1837', in BLAGG, THOMAS M., & FARROW, MARGARET A., eds. *N.P.R.M.* **12**, *P.P.R.S.* **237**. Phillimore, 1936, 39-43.

Ingworth

JOHNSON, FRED., ed. 'Marriages at Ingworth, 1559 to 1812', in PHILLIMORE, W.P.W., & JOHNSON, FREDERIC, eds. *N.P.R.M.* **1**, *P.P.R.S.* **9**. Phillimore, 1899, 97-103.

Kirstead

P., A.T. 'Simames in parish registers', *East Anglian* **1**, 1864, 118-9. Lists surnames in the registers of Kirstead with Langhale, Norfolk, 1663-1799.

Lakenham

WESTGATE, PAULINE. 'Jottings from the baptism registers of Old Lakenham, Norwich', *N.Anc.* **6**(6), 1992, 194. Brief note.

Lammas

RYE, WALTER, ed. *The first register book of the parish of Lammas and Little Hautbois in the county of Norfolk, with some notes from later registers.* Norwich: Gibbs & Waller, 1905.

Langford

FARROW, CHARLES W., ed. *Langford, 1692-1837.* P.R.N. **18**, 1987. Includes census schedules, 1841-81.

Langhale

See Kirstead

Langham

FINLAYSON, W.H., ed. 'Marriages at Langham Episcopi 1695 to 1812', in PHILLIMORE, W.P.W., & JOHNSON, FREDERIC, eds. *N.P.R.M.* **3**, *P.P.R.S.* **75**. Phillimore, 1907, 141-46.

Langley

'Marriages at Langley, 1695 to 1812', in PHILLIMORE, W.P.W., & JOHNSON, FREDERIC, eds. *N.P.R.M.* **1**, *P.P.R.S.* **9**. Phillimore, 1899, 133-40.

Leziate

See Ashwicken

Litcham

BLOOM, J. HARVEY, ed. 'Marriages at Litcham, 1555 to 1812', in PHILLIMORE, W.P.W., JOHNSON, FREDERIC, & BLOOM, J. HARVEY, eds. *N.P.R.M.* **2**, *P.P.R.S.* **13**. Phillimore, 1900, 33-51. See also *N.P.R.M.* **10**, *P.P.R.S.* **225**. Phillimore, 1916, 183.

Little Cressingham

FARROW, C.W., ed. *Little Cressingham, 1691-1837.* P.R.N. **20**, 1987.

Little Hautbois

See Lamas

Little Massingham

BRERETON, H.L., ed. 'Marriages at Little Massingham, 1559 to 1837', in ASTLEY, H.J. DUKINFIELD, ed. *N.P.R.M.* **8**, *P.P.R.S.* **202**. Phillimore, 1914, 141-9.

Little Melton

EDMONDS, JENIFER, ed. *Little Melton 1734-1837.* P.R.N. **28**, 1989. Includes list of clergy.

Little Plumstead

DAVENEY, H. 'Extracts from parish registers, no.4: Plumstead Parva', *East Anglian* **1**, 1864, 305-6.

Little Snoring

JOHNSON, F., & MARTIN, W., eds. 'Marriages at
Snoring Parva, 1559 to 1837', in PHILLIMORE,
W.P.W. & BLAGG, THOS. M., eds. *N.P.R.M.* **6**,
P.P.R.S. **157**. Phillimore, 1912, 71-85.

Marsham

MICHELL, A.T., ed. *The parish register of
Marsham, Norfolk, from 1538 to 1836.*
Norwich: Jarrold & Sons, 1889. Includes list of
rectors.

Mattishall

SEAMAN, PETER J., ed. *Mattishall & Dereham
Congregational, 1772-1837; Mattishall &
Walton Primitive Methodist, 1832-1837.* N.N.R.
1, 1983.

Mautby

HOLLEY, G.H., ed. 'Marriages at Mautby, 1663 to
1834', in PHILLIMORE, W.P.W., & HOLLEY, G.H.,
eds. *N.P.R.M.* **5**, *P.P.R.S.* **148**. Phillimore, 1910,
105-9.

Middleton

DAUBENEY, A.R.V., ed. 'Marriages at Middleton,
1560 to 1837', in his *N.P.R.M.* **10**, *P.P.R.S.* **225**.
Phillimore, 1916, 105-37.

Mundsley

HARVEY, J. TEGG, ed. 'Marriages at Mundesley,
1724 to 1812', in PHILLIMORE, W.P.W., &
JOHNSON, FREDERIC, eds. *N.P.R.M.* **3**, *P.P.R.S.*
75. Phillimore, 1907, 147-50.

Narborough

BLOOM, J. HARVEY, ed. 'Marriages at Narborough,
1558 to 1812', in PHILLIMORE, W.P.W., &
JOHNSON, FREDERIC, eds. *N.P.R.M.* **1**, *P.P.R.S.* **9**.
Phillimore, 1899, 1899, 141-53.

Narford

BLOOM, J. HARVEY, ed. 'Marriages at Narford,
1559 to 1812', in PHILLIMORE, W.P.W., JOHNSON,
FREDERIC, & BLOOM, J. HARVEY, eds. *N.P.R.M.* **2**,
P.P.R.S. **13**. Phillimore, 1900, 5-9.

North Barsham

WHALL, E.H., ed. 'Marriages at North Barsham,
1557 to 1837', in PHILLIMORE, W.P.W., & BLAGG,
THOS. M., eds. *N.P.R.M.* **6**, *P.P.R.S.* **157**.
Phillimore, 1912, 49-60.

North Elmham

LEGGE, AUGUSTUS GEORGE, ed. *The ancient
register of North Elmham, Norfolk, from A.D.
1538 to A.D. 1831.* Norwich: A.H. Goose &
Co., 1888. Includes notes on families and some
extracts from later registers.

North Runcton

DAUBENEY, A.R.V., ed. 'Marriages at North
Runcton, with hamlets of Setchey and
Hardwick, 1563 to 1837', in his *N.P.R.M.* **11**,
P.P.R.S. **232**. Phillimore, 1926, 95-117.

Northwold

PEARSON, W.M.C. *Extracts from parish registers:
Northwold, Co.Norfolk'*, East Anglian N.S. **5**,
1893-4, 91-3. Brief.

North Wotton

LEWIS, R.W.M., ed. 'Marriages at North Wotton,
1655 to 1837', in his *N.P.R.M.* **9**, *P.P.R.S.* **215**.
Phillimore, 1914, 99-107.

Norwich

FONE, JOHN F. *Index to Norwich marriages, 1813-
1837.* Norfolk genealogy **14**, 1982. Covers all
35 Norwich parishes, the Norfolk Society of
Friends registers, and a few strays. For some
Roman Catholic additions, see:

PALGRAVE-MOORE, PATRICK. 'Roman Catholic
marriages in Norwich', *N.Anc.* **3**(5), 1984, 7.

Cathedral

JOHNSON, FREDERIC, & BOLINGBROKE, L.G., eds.
*Marriages recorded in the register of the sacrist
of the Cathedral church of Norwich, 1697-1754*
transcribed by T.R. Tallack. Norwich: Agas H.
Goose for the Norfolk and Norwich
Archaeological Society, [1902].

Dutch Church

MOENS, W.J.C., ed. 'Register of the Dutch
Reformed Church, Norwich', *East Anglian* N.S.
1, 1885-6, 118-9, 133-4, 141-2, 192-4 & 205-6.
'The Norwich Dutch church: early register of
baptisms, 1598-1619', *East Anglian* N.S. **12**,
1907-8, passim; **13**, 1909-10, passim. A full
index to the register is printed in Moens work
listed in section 14.

Old Meeting House

BROWN, A. STUART. 'Baptisms recorded in the
church book of the Old Meeting House,
Norwich, 1657-1681', *N.R.S.* **22**, 1951, 5-9.

St.Clement

See St.Michael at Thorn

St.George at Tombland

JAY, G.B., ET AL, eds. *The first parish register of
St.George of Tombland, Norwich, A.D. 1538-
1707.* Nowich: A.H. Goose, 1891.

Norwich *continued*
St.Mary at Coslany
BOLINGBROKE, L.G., & JOHNSON, FREDERIC, eds. 'Marriages at St.Mary Coslany, Norwich, 1557 to 1812', in PHILLIMORE, W.P.W., & JOHNSON, FREDERIC, eds. *N.P.R.M.* **3**, *P.P.R.S.* **75**. Phillimore, 1907, 1-52.

St.Michael at Plea
TALLACK, THOMAS R., ed. *The first parish register of St.Michael-at-Plea, Norwich, A.D. 1538-1695*. Norwich: [ ], 1892.

FARROW, C.W. 'The first parish register of St.Michael at Plea, Norwich, A.D. 1538-1695, transcribed by Thomas R. Tallack, 1892', *Suffolk roots* **3**(1), 1977, 52-3. Suffolk strays only.

St.Michael at Thorn
'Extracts from parish registers, no.10', *East Anglian* **2**, 1866, 306-7. From St.Michaels at Thorne, Norwich, and St.Clements, Fyebridge, Norwich. Brief.

Oby
HOLLEY, G.H., ed. 'Marriages at Oby, 1563 to 1718', in PHILLIMORE, W.P.W., & HOLLEY, G.H., eds. *N.P.R.M.* **7**, *P.P.R.S.* **179**. Phillimore, 1912, 135-7.

See also Thurne

Old Buckenham
RYE, W., ed. *The first register book of the parish of Old Buckenham in Norfolk, 1560 to 1649*. Norwich: A.H. Goose, 1902.

Ormsby St.Margaret
HOLLEY, G.H., ed. 'Marriages at Ormesby St.Margaret (with Scratby) 1601 to 1837', in PHILLIMORE, W.P.W., & HOLLEY, G.H., eds. *N.P.R.M.* **7**, *P.P.R.S.* **179**. Phillimore, 1912, 41-70.

Paston
EXTRANEOUS. 'Extracts from parish registers, no.5: Paston, Norfolk', *East Anglian* **1**, 1864, 379-80. Brief.

Pentney
DAUBENEY, A.R. VAUGHAN, ed. 'Marriages at Pentney, 1731 to 1837', in his *N.P.R.M.* **10**, *P.P.R.S.* **225**. Phillimore, 1916, 65-74.

Rackheath
FARROW, C.W., ed. *Rackheath, 1645-1837*. P.R.N. **1**, 1984.

Ranworth
CHOLMELEY, H. WALDO, ed. 'Marriages at Ranworth, 1559 to 1812', in PHILLIMORE, W.P.W., & JOHNSON, FREDERIC, eds. *N.P.R.M.* **3**, *P.P.R.S.* **75**. Phillimore, 1907, 85-97.

Redenhall
RAYSON, GEORGE. 'Extracts from parish registers, no.32: Redenhall with Harleston, Norfolk', *East Anglian* **4**, 1871, 150-52. Brief.

Roxham
See Ryston

Roydon by Lynn
FARROW, C.W., ed. *Roydon, 1559-1837*. P.R.N. **26**, 1988.

Roydon by Diss
LEWIS, R.W.M., ed. 'Marriages at Roydon, 1721 to 1837', in LEWIS, R.W.M., ed. *N.P.R.M.* **9**, *P.P.R.S.* **215**. Phillimore, 1914, 77-82.

Runham
HOLLEY, G. HUNT, ed. 'Marriages at Runham, 1538 to 1812', in PHILLIMORE, W.P.W., & HOLLEY, G.H., eds. *N.P.R.M.* **5**, *P.P.R.S.* **148**. Phillimore, 1910, 37-45.

Runton
'Notes on Runton, Norfolk: parish registers, the church, charities, &c.', *N.A.M.* **1**, 1877, 420-33. Includes brief extracts from the parish register, a few monumental inscriptions, brief list of rectors, etc.

Rushall
'Surnames in parish registers: Rushall, Norfolk', *East Anglian* **2**, 1866, 314-6. List, 1561-1800.

Ryston
PALGRAVE-MOORE, PATRICK, ed. *Ryston cum Roxham, 1687-1837*. P.R.N. **7**, 1986.

Santon
FARROW, C.W., ed. *Santon, 1707-1837, with census returns, 1841-1881*. P.R.N. **16**, 1986.

Saxlingham Thorpe
GOLDSMITH, WENDY, ed. *Saxlingham Thorpe Particular Baptist: births and registrations, 1793-1837. N.N.R.* **7**, 1989.

Sco Ruston
ROWLES, STUART, ed. *Sco Ruston, 1707-1837*. P.R.N. **30**, 1989.

Scratby
See Ormsby St.Margaret

Sculthorpe

BLAGG, T.M., & LABOUCHERE, J.A., eds. 'Marriages at Sculthorpe, 1561 to 1837', in PHILLIMORE, W.P.W., & BLAGG, THOS. M., eds. *N.P.R.M.* **6**, *P.P.R.S.* **157**. Phillimore, 1912, 135-53.

Sedgford

LEWIS, R.W.M., & FARROW, M.A., eds. 'Marriages at Sedgeford, 1560 to 1837', in BLAGG, THOMAS M., & FARROW, MARGARET A., eds. *N.P.R.M.* **12**, *P.P.R.S.* **237**. Phillimore, 1936, 49-74.

Setchey

See North Runcton

Shelfanger

FARROW, C.W., ed. *Shelfanger, 1686-1837.* P.R.N. **25**, 1988.

BODLE, A.N., ed. *Shelfanger Particular Baptist Chapel births, 1795-1837. N.N.R.* **4**, 1987.

Shelton

P., G.R. 'Surnames in parish registers, no.5: Shelton, Norfolk', *East Anglian* **4**, 1871, 214-6. List, 1557-1800.

RAYSON, GEORGE. 'Extracts from parish registers, no.35: Shelton, Norfolk', *East Anglian* **4**, 1871, 256-8. Brief.

Shereford

HUGHES, F. HAWKER, ed. 'Marriages at Shereford, 1722 to 1837', in ASTLEY, H.J. DUKINFIELD, ed. *N.P.R.M.* **8**, *P.P.R.S.* **202**. Phillimore, 1914, 109-12.

Shernborne

LEWIS, R.W.M., ed. 'Marriages at Shernborne, 1755 to 1838', in BLAGG, THOMAS M., & FARROW, MARGARET, A., eds. *N.P.R.M.* **12**, *P.P.R.S.* **237**. Phillimore, 1936, 45-7.

Shingham

FARROW, C.W., ed. *Shingham, 1708-1837.* P.R.N. **5**, 1985.

Sidestrand

HOARE, CHRISTOBEL M. *Records of a Norfolk village: being notes on the parish of Sidestrand; with a complete transcript of the registers, 1558-1858.* Bedford: Times Publishing, 1914. Includes monumental inscriptions, extracts from the Town Book, brief family histories, etc.

Smallburgh

'Extracts from parish registers, no.13: Smallburgh, Norfolk', *East Anglian* **2**, 1866, 134. See also 154. Brief; few names.

Snettisham

BLOOM, J. HARVEY, ed. 'Marriages at Snettisham, 1682 to 1812', in PHILLIMORE, W.P.W., JOHNSON, FREDERIC, & BLOOM, J. HARVEY, eds. *N.P.R.M.* **2**, *P.P.R.S.* **13**. Phillimore, 1900, 105-27.

South Acre

BLOOM, J. HARVEY, ed. 'Marriages at Southacre, 1576 to 1812', in PHILLIMORE, W.P.W., & JOHNSON, FREDERIC, eds. *N.R.P.M.* **1**, *P.P.R.S.* **9**. Phillimore, 1899, 105-12.

South Creake

BLAGG, T.M., ET AL, eds. 'Marriages at South Creake, 1559 to 1837', in ASTLEY, H.J. DUKINFIELD, ed. *N.P.R.M.* **8**, *P.P.R.S.* **202**. Phillimore, 1914, 75-105.

Southmere

See Docking

South Raynham

ASTLEY, DUKINFIELD, ed. 'Marriages at South Rainham, 1601 to 1837', in DAUBENEY, A.R. VAUGHAN, ed. *N.P.R.M.* **11**, *P.P.R.S.* **232**. Phillimore, 1926, 143-50.

South Walsham. St.Lawrence

'Extracts from parish registers, no.2: South Walsham, St.Lawrence', *East Anglian* **1**, 1864, 175-78. Includes list of those who signed the Solemn League and Covenant, 1643.

South Wooton

LEWIS, R.W.M., ed. 'Marriages at South Wooton, 1556 to 1837', in his *N.P.R.M.* **9**, *P.P.R.S.* **215**. Phillimore, 1914, 109-25.

Stanford

FARROW, C.W., ed. *Stanford with Sturston, 1699-1837.* P.R.N. **22**, 1987.

Stanhoe

'Marriages at Stanhow with Barwick, 1567 to 1837', in BLAGG, THOMAS M., & FARROW, MARGARET A., eds. *N.P.R.M.* **12**, *P.P.R.S.* **237**. Phillimore, 1936, 109-27.

Stokesby

HOLLEY, GEORGE HUNT, ed. 'Marriages at Stokesby with Herringsby, 1560 to 1812', in PHILLIMORE, W.P.W., & HOLLEY, G.H., eds. *N.P.R.M.* **5**, *P.P.R.S.* **148**. Phillimore, 1910, 1-13.

Stratton St.Michael

GOLDSMITH, WENDY, ed. *Stratton St.Michael Congregational: births and baptisms, 1825-1837. N.N.R.* **6**, 1989.

Strumpshaw

JOHNSON, F., ed. 'Marriages at Strumpshaw, 1562 to 1812', in PHILLIMORE, W.P.W., & JOHNSON, FREDERIC, eds. *N.P.R.M.* **1**, *P.P.R.S.* **9**. Phillimore, 1899, 77-88.

Sturston

See Stanford

Swaffham

DAUBENEY, A.R. VAUGHAN, ed. 'Marriages at Swaffham, 1559 to 1837', in his *N.P.R.M.* **11**, *P.P.R.S.* **232**. Phillimore, 1926, 1-93.

Syderstone

ASTLEY, H.J. DUKINFIELD. 'Extracts from the two oldest registers of the parish of Syderstone, Norfolk', *N.A.* **15**, 1904, 196-226.

BLAGG, T.M., & WILLAEY, H.G., eds. 'Marriages at Syderstone, 1585 to 1837', in ASTLEY, H.J. DUKINFIELD, ed. *N.P.R.M.* **8**, *P.P.R.S.* **202**. Phillimore, 1914, 57-73.

Tatterford

BLAGG, T.M., & JONES, R.W. INIGO, eds. 'Marriages at Tatterford, 1561 to 1837', in PHILLIMORE, W.P.W., & BLAGG, THOS. M., eds. *N.P.R.M.* **6**, *P.P.R.S.* **157**. Phillimore, 1912, 117-27.

Tatterset

BLAGG, T.M., ed. 'Marriages at Tattersett, 1755 to 1837', in PHILLIMORE, W.P.W., & BLAGG, THOS. M., eds. *N.P.R.M.* **6**, *P.P.R.S.* **157**. Phillimore, 1912, 129-33.

Taverham

SIMS, JUDITH M., ed. *Taverham, 1601-1837*. P.R.N. **8**, 1986.

Terrington St.John

GREER, SANDY, ET AL, eds. *Terrington Scti Johns in the County of Norfolk: the register book of all ye christenings, marriages and burials from Candlemas in the year of our lord 1538*. 3 vols. Wisbech: Seagull Enterprises, 1985-[8]. v.1. 1538-1600. v.2. 1601-1650. v.3. 1651-1700.

Threxton

PALGRAVE-MOORE, PATRICK, ed. *Threxton 1602/3-1837*. P.R.N. **4**, 1985. Includes monumental inscriptions.

Thrigby

HOLLEY, GEO. HUNT, ed. 'Marriages at Thrigby, 1539 to 1812', in PHILLIMORE, W.P.W., & HOLLEY, G.H., eds. *N.P.R.M.* **5**, *P.P.R.S.* **148**. Phillimore, 1910, 71-5.

Thurne

HOLLEY, G.H., ed. 'Marriages at Thurne with Oby and Ashby, 1559 to 1837', in PHILLIMORE, W.P.W. & HOLLEY, G.H., eds. *N.P.R.M.* **7**, *P.P.R.S.* **179**. Phillimore, 1912, 139-49.

Thursford

JOHNSON, FRED., ed. 'Marriages at Thursford, 1692 to 1837', in PHILLIMORE, W.P.W., & BLAGG, THOS. M., eds. *N.P.R.M.* **6**, *P.P.R.S.* **157**. Phillimore, 1912, 107-15.

Thwaite

TAYLOR, R. FETZER, ed. 'Marriages at Thwaite St.Mary, 1539 to 1837', in PHILLIMORE, W.P.W., & HOLLEY, G.H., eds. *N.P.R.M.* **5**, *P.P.R.S.* **148**. Phillimore, 1910, 129-35.

Toft Monks

ASHBY, A.J. 'Extracts from the parish registers of Toft Monks, Norfolk', *East Anglian* N.S. **3**, 1889-90, 7-10. General discussion, with few extracts.

Toftrees

GWYN, CECIL. 'Marriages at Toftrees, 1754 to 1834', in PHILLIMORE, W.P.W., & BLAGG, THOS. M., eds. *N.P.R.M.* **6**, *P.P.R.S.* **157**. Phillimore, 1912, 43-7.

Topcroft

TAYLOR, R. FETZER, ed. 'Marriages at Topcroft, 1557 to 1813', in PHILLIMORE, W.P.W., & HOLLEY, G.H., eds. *N.P.R.M.* **5**, *P.P.R.S.* **148**. Phillimore, 1910, 111-28.

Tuttington

'Extracts from the parish registers of Tuttington, Co.Norfolk', *Genealogist* N.S. **11**, 1895, 128.

Upton

JOHNSON, FRED., ed. 'Marriages at Upton, 1558 to 1812', in PHILLIMORE, W.P.W., & JOHNSON, FREDERIC, eds. *N.P.R.M.* **1**, *P.P.R.S.* **9**. Phillimore, 1899, 51-65.

Walpole

'Walpole registers', *F.N.Q.* **7**, 1907-9, 67-70. 18th c. extracts.

Walpole St.Peter

HOWMAN, EDWD. J. 'Extracts from parish registers, no.26: Walpole St.Peter', *East Anglian* **3**, 1869, 167-9. Brief.

Walton

See Mattishall

Waterden

ASTLEY, H.J.D., ed. 'Marriages at Waterden, 1743 to 1812', in ASTLEY, H.J. DUKINFIELD, ed. *N.P.R.M.* **8**, *P.P.R.S.* **202**. Phillimore, 1914, 107-8.

Watton

'The old parish registers of Watton', *N.N.N.Q.* 1st series, 1896-9, 278-80. General discussion.

Weasenham All Saints

BURROWS, GLYNN. 'An index of names in the baptismal register of Weasenham All Saints and in the marriage registers of Weasenham All Saints and Weasenham St.Peter', *N.Anc.* 2(4), 1981, 47-8. 18-19th c.

Weasenham St.Peter

See Weasenham All Saints

Weeting

ORAM, R.A., ed. 'Marriages at Weeting', in PHILLIMORE, W.P.W., & JOHNSON, FREDERIC, eds. *N.P.R.M.* **4**, *P.P.R.S.* **95**. Phillimore, 1909, 39-66. Covers 1558-1812.

West Acre

DAUBENEY, A.R. VAUGHAN, ed. 'Marriages at Westacre, 1665 to 1837', in his *N.P.R.M.* **10**, *P.P.R.S.* **225**. Phillimore, 1916, 33-49.

West Barsham

MARTIN, W., ed. 'Marriages at West Barsham, 1813 to 1837', in PHILLIMORE, W.P.W., & BLAGG, THOS. M., eds. *N.P.R.M.* **6**, *P.P.R.S.* **157**. Phillimore, 1912, 69.

West Beckham

JERVIS, E.C., ed. 'Marriages at West Beckham, 1689 to 1836', in PHILLIMORE, W.P.W., & JOHNSON, FREDERIC, eds. *N.P.R.M.* **3**, *P.P.R.S.* **75**. Phillimore, 1907, 135-9.

West Bilney

DAUBENEY, A.R. VAUGHAN, ed. 'Marriages at West Bilney, 1562 to 1838', in his *N.P.R.M.* **10**, *P.P.R.S.* **225**. Phillimore, 1916, 75-86.

West Newton

BLOOM, J. HARVEY, ET AL, eds. 'Marriages at West Newton, 1561 to 1837', in PHILLIMORE, W.P.W., & HOLLEY, G.H., eds. *N.P.R.M.* **5**, *P.P.R.S.* **148**. Phillimore, 1910, 137-49.

West Raynham

BLAGG, T.M., & ASTLEY, DR., eds. 'Marriages at West Rainham, 1538 to 1764', in DAUBENEY, A.R. VAUGHAN, ed. *N.P.R.M.* **11**, *P.P.R.S.* **232**. Phillimore, 1926, 119-24.

West Rudham

BLAGG, T.M., ed. 'Marriages at West Rudham, 1565 to 1837', in ASTLEY, H.J. DUKINFIELD, ed. *N.P.R.M.* **8**, *P.P.R.S.* **202**. Phillimore, 1914, 21-42.

West Somerton

HOLLEY, G.H., ed. 'Marriages at West Somerton, 1737 to 1837', in PHILLIMORE, W.P.W., & HOLLEY, G.H., eds. *N.P.R.M.* **7**, *P.P.R.S.* **179**. Phillimore, 1912, 129-33.

West Tofts

FARROW, C.W., ed. *West Tofts with Buckenham Tofts, 1705-1837*. P.R.N. **21**, 1987.

Weybourne

'An index of Weybourne marriages, 1800-1850', *N.Anc.* 3(5), 1984, 70.

Whissonsett

WILLIAMS, J.F., & SEAGRIM, C.P.C., eds. 'Marriages at Whissonsett, 1700 to 1837', in ASTLEY, H.J. DUKINFIELD, ed. *N.P.R.M.* **8**, *P.P.R.S.* **202**. Phillimore, 1914, 129-40.

Winterton

'Marriages at Winterton with East Somerton, 1747 to 1837', in PHILLIMORE, W.P.W., & HOLLEY, G.H., eds. *N.P.R.M.* **7**, *P.P.R.S.* **179**. Phillimore, 1912, 119-28.

Witton

JOHNSON, FRed., ed. 'Marriages at Witton by Blofield, 1582 to 1812', in PHILLIMORE, W.P.W., & JOHNSON, FREDERIC, eds. *N.P.R.M.* **1**, *P.P.R.S.* **9**. Phillimore, 1899, 67-71.

Wolferton

BLOOM, J.H., ed. 'Marriages at Wolferton, 1653 to 1812', in PHILLIMORE, W.P.W., JOHNSON, FREDERIC, & BLOOM, J. HARVEY, eds. *N.P.R.M.* **2**, *P.P.R.S.* **13**. Phillimore, 1900, 99-103.

Woodbastwick

CHOLMELEY, H. WALDO, ed. 'Marriages at Woodbastwick, 1561 to 1812', in PHILLIMORE, W.P.W., & JOHNSON, FREDERIC, eds. *N.P.R.M.* **3**, *P.P.R.S.* **75**. Phillimore, 1907, 99-116.

Woodton

TAYLOR, R. FETZER, ed. 'Marriages at Woodton, 1538 to 1812', in PHILLIMORE, W.P.W., & HOLLEY, G.H., eds. *N.P.R.M.* **5**, *P.P.R.S.* **148**. Phillimore, 1910, 47-60.

9. MONUMENTAL INSCRIPTIONS

A. *GENERAL*

Monumental inscriptions are an important source of genealogical information, especially for the last two or three centuries. Their transcription has been an important part of the work of the Norfolk and Norwich Genealogical Society. A list of both printed and manuscript transcripts of inscriptions then in existence is given in:

PALGRAVE-MOORE, P. 'Norfolk memorial inscriptions', *N.Anc.* **1**(1), 1977, 11-13. This list is regularly updated in *N.Anc.*

For an earlier list of transcripts covering Cambridgeshire and Suffolk as well as Norfolk, see:

MARSHALL, G.W. 'Monumental inscriptions', *East Anglian* **1**, 1864, 367-9, 399-401 & 431-6. See also **2**, 1866, 117.

General studies of Norfolk monumental inscriptions include:

LINNELL, C.L.S., & WEARING, STANLEY J. *Norfolk church monuments.* Ipswich: Norman Adland & Co., 1952. Includes biographical notes on persons commemorated, with a list of sculptors.

MARSDEN, WALTER. *Resting places in East Anglia.* Romford: Henry, 1987. Guide to burial places of 'worthies'.

MARSHALL, GEORGE W. 'Monumental inscriptions from some churches in Norfolk, etc.', *East Anglian* **3**, 1868, 320-39. From many churches. Includes parish register extracts. Also covers Debden, Essex, and Stapleford, Cambridgeshire.

RYE, WALTER. *Early recumbent figures on monuments in Norfolk before 1500.* Rye's Norfolk handlists, 1st series **6**. Norwich: Roberts & Co., 1916.

RYE, WALTER. *Some early English inscriptions in Norfolk before 1600, mostly from (1) churches, monuments and windows, pulpits, doors, and seats, but also from (2) houses, fire-places, etc., etc., to which are added, lists of local miracles and martyrs* ... Jarrolds, [1923]. Includes 187 inscriptions.

'[Monumental inscriptions in various Norfolk churches]', *Fragmenta Genealogica* **9**, 1903, passim.

For war memorials, see:

War memorials in North Norfolk. Holt: K. Fletcher, 1991.

Monumental Inscriptions continued

A. GENERAL continued

Two recent studies of Norfolk brasses are:

GREENWOOD, ROGER, & NORRIS, MALCOLM. *The brasses of Norfolk churches*. Woodbridge: Norfolk Churches Trust, 1976.

SPINKS, WINIFRed. *A memento from old England*. Bardwell: the author, 1977. A study of brasses in Norfolk and Suffolk, etc.

An important older study is:

FARRER, EDMUND. *A list of monumental brasses remaining in the county of Norfolk, MDCCCXC*. Norwich: A.H. Goose, 1890.

This is supplemented by:

FARRER, EDMUND. 'List of some brasses in Norfolk churches', *N.A.* **13**, 1898, 192-8.

RYE, WALTER. 'Norfolk brasses', *East Anglian* N.S. **5**, 1893-4, 161-4. See also 209-10.

Many brasses were noted in Blomefield's *History of Norfolk* (see above section 1). Some that were not are recorded in:

MANNING, C.R. 'Monumental brass inscriptions in Norfolk omitted in Blomefield's history of the county', *N.A.* **10**, 1888, 192-224; **11**, 1892, 72-104.

Other studies include:

BELOE, E.M. *A series of photo-lithographs of monumental brasses and matrices of the fourteenth and fifteenth centuries now or formerly existing in the County of Norfolk*. Kings Lynn: W. Griggs, 1890-91.

CLARK, H.O. 'An eighteenth-century record of Norfolk sepulchral brasses', *N.A.* **26**, 1938, 85-102. Lists 100 brasses.

COTMAN, JOHN SELL. *Engravings of sepulchral brasses in Norfolk and Suffolk: tending to illustrate the ecclesiastical, military and civil costume as well as to preserve memorials of ancient families in that county*. 2nd ed. Henry G. Bohn, 1838.

DRAKE, WILLIAM. 'Sepulchral brasses: notices of interesting memorials in Norfolk and other counties', *Archaeological journal* **2**, 1845, 243-50. Includes a list of Warwickshire brasses.

MANNING, C.R. 'Lost brasses', *N.A.* **6**, 1864, 3-26.

STEPHENSON, MILL. 'A list of palimpsest brasses: Norfolk', *Transactions of the Monumental Brass Society* **4**, 1900-1903, 219-45.

STEPHENSON, MILL. 'Palimpsest brasses in Norfolk', *N.A.* **15**, 1904, 61-90.

CLARK, H.O. 'More Norfolk palimpsest brasses', *N.A.* **22**, 1926, 59-74.

For heraldry, see section 10 below.

B. BY PLACE

Acle

See Swafield

Appleton

M., G.W. 'Monumental inscriptions: Appleton church, Norfolk', *East Anglian* **1**, 1864, 169.

Bacton

A. 'Monumental inscriptions in Bacton church, Norfolk', *East Anglian* **1**, 1864, 328-9.

Banham

PALGRAVE-MOORE, PATRICK. 'An index of surnames on monumental inscriptions at Banham', *N.Anc.* **2**(5), 1981, 67.

Bawburgh

MINNS, MR. & MRS., & HEMSTED, JOHN. 'An index of memorial and monumental inscriptions at Bawburgh', *N.Anc.* **2**(6), 1981, 78.

Bergh Apton

HEMSTED, JOHN. 'An index of monumental inscriptions at Bergh Apton', *N.Anc.* **2**(7), 1981, 87.

Breckles Deanery

PEDOMETER. 'Church heraldry: deaneries of Breccles and Redenhall', *Eastern Counties collectanea*, 1872/3, 52-288 passim.

Brockdish

'Monumental inscriptions at Brockdish: index of surnames', *N.Anc.* **2**(9), 1982, 118.

Buckenham

See Burlingham

Burlingham

'Some more Norfolk monumental inscriptions', *N.Anc.* **3**(6), 1984, 83-4. Surname index for inscriptions at Burlingham North St.Andrews, Burlingham South St.Edmund, and Buckenham Ferry.

Buxton

PIKE, CHRISTOPHER S. 'Monumental inscriptions from disused Baptist chapel, Buxton', *N.Anc.* **5**(5), 1989, 107.

Cley Next The Sea

LINNELL, C.L.S. 'The brasses at Cley-next-the-Sea', *Transactions of the Monumental Brass Society* **8**, 1943-51, 196-202.

Cringleford

PALGRAVE-MOORE, PATRICK. 'An index of memorial inscriptions at Cringleford', *N.Anc.* **1**(3), 1978, 31-3.

B. *BY PLACE continued*

Cromer

RYE, WALTER. 'Inscriptions in Cromer church and churchyard', *East Anglian* 2, 1866, 301-3. 37 monumental inscriptions.

Eaton

PALGRAVE-MOORE, PATRICK, & HEMSTED, JOHN. 'An index of memorial inscriptions at Eaton', *N.Anc.* 1(9), 1979, 114-5.

Edingthorpe

See Swafield

Felbrigg Hall

THOMAS, JOAN A. 'Heraldry at Felbrigg Hall', *Norfolk Standard* 1, 1977, 108-9. Brief note.

Framingham Earl

MINNS, F. 'Framingham Earl: an index of names taken from the monumental inscriptions', *N.Anc.* 2(10), 1982, 129.

Framingham Pigot

PALGRAVE-MOORE, PATRICK, & MINNS, F. 'Framingham Pigot: an index of names taken from the monumental inscriptions', *N.Anc.* 2(10), 1982, 129.

Great Yarmouth

SIMPSON, JUSTIN. 'Monumental heraldry of Yarmouth, &c.', *East Anglian* 2, 1866, 269-70, 283-5 & 309.

TURNER, DAWSON. *Sepulchral reminiscences of a market town, as afforded by a list of the interments within the walls of the parish church of St.Nicholas, Great Yarmouth, collected chiefly from monuments & grave-stones still remaining, June 1845.* Yarmouth: C. Barber, 1848.

'Great Yarmouth tombstones', *E.A.M.* **1935**, 50-51 & 52. List.

Gressenhall

CARRINGTON, A.C., ET AL. *A record of the monumental inscriptions in the church and churchyard of St.Mary, Gressenhall, Norfolk.* Gressenhall: Gressenhall News and Views, 1981.

Hardley

M., G.W. 'Monumental inscriptions in Hardley church, Norfolk', *East Anglian* 1, 1864, 234.

Heigham

WILLIAMS, J.F. 'The brasses of Heigham church, Norwich', *Transactions of the Monumental Brass Society* 8, 1943-51, 145-7.

Happing Hundred

RYE, WALTER. *The monumental inscriptions in the Hundred of Happing in the county of Norfolk.* Norwich: Goose & Co., 1886.

Hindolveston

ANDRE, J. LEWIS. 'Hindolvestone church, Norfolk', *Reliquary* N.S. 7, 1893, 28-33. Includes monumental inscriptions.

Hockwold

See Wilton

Holt Hundred

DEW, WALTON N. *The monumental inscriptions in the Hundred of Holt, in the County of Norfolk.* ed. Walter Rye. Norwich: A.H. Goose & Co., 1885.

Hoveton St.John

See Swafield

Hunstanton

'Monumental inscriptions in the church of St.Mary, the Virgin, Hunstanton', *East Anglian* 2, 1866, 220-22. See also 249.

Kings Lynn

BELOE, E.M. 'A list of brasses existing in the churches of St.Margaret and St.Nicholas, Kings Lynn, in the year 1724', *Transactions of the Monumental Brass Society* 2, 1899, 57-9.

CAMERON, H.K. 'The fourteenth-century Flemish brasses at Kings Lynn', *Archaeological journal* **136**, 1979, 151-72.

EDLESTON, R.H. 'Monumental inscriptions in St.Margaret's church, Lynn', *F.N.Q.* 1, 1889-91, 77-81, 115-6, 182-8, 207-11 & 282.

HOVELL, ETHEL M.W. *A complete list of the inscriptions on the slabs, tablets and monuments in the chapel of St.Nicholas, King's Lynn, existing in the year 1937.* Kings Lynn: G.R. Oswell & Son, 1937.

Lakenham

PALGRAVE-MOORE, PATRICK, & HEMSTED, JOHN. 'An index of memorial and monumental inscriptions at Lakenham', *N.Anc.* 2(3), 1980, 37-8.

Langley

MARSHALL, GEORGE W. 'Langley, Norfolk', *East Anglian* 2, 1866, 279-80, 291-2 & 299-300. Monumental inscriptions and heraldry.

B. *BY PLACE continued*
Langley Abbey
DENT, JOHN. 'Heraldry at Langley Abbey', *Norfolk Standard* 3(6), 1983, 90-91 & 96.

Little Walsingham
BOND, H.A. 'The brasses at Little Walsingham, Norfolk', *N.A.* **33**, 1965, 450-56. 23 inscriptions.

EVANS, H.F. OWEN. 'A find of palimpsests at Little Walsingham, Norfolk', *Transactions of the Monumental Brass Society* **10**(82), 1965, 204-9.

Narborough
M., G. 'Notes on Narburgh church, Norfolk', *Topographer and Genealogist* **2**, 1853, 224-33. Monumental inscriptions.

New Buckenham
See Old Buckenham

North Burlingham
WYLAM, A.R.B. 'Monumental inscriptions in North Burlingham, St.Peter', *N.A.* **32**, 1961, 82-4.

North Walsham
RYE, WALTER. 'North Walsham church, Norfolk', *East Anglian* **3**, 1869, 235-40. Notes on 100 monumental inscriptions.

Northwold
PEARSON, WM. C. 'Monumental inscriptions in Northwold church', *East Anglian* N.S. **5**, 1893-4, 26-8.

Norton Subcourse
M., G.W. 'Monumental inscriptions in church of Norton-Subcourse, Co.Norfolk', *East Anglian* **1**, 1864, 301.

Norwich
'Monumental inscriptions at Norwich', *Genealogist* N.S. **1**, 1884, 38-42.

'Norwich church notes', *Fragmenta Genealogica* **3**, 1897, 1-28. Inscriptions from various parishes.

'Suffolk monumental inscriptions in the city of Norwich', *East Anglian* N.S. **2**, 1887-8, 84-6, 101-3 & 198-200.

Cathedral
ALDRED, M.C. 'Some of the memorials in Norwich Cathedral', *Monumental journal* **31**, 1957, 31-7.

BROWNE, SIR THOMAS. *Repertorium, or, some account of the tombs and monuments in the Cathedral church of Norwich, begun by Sir Thomas Browne, and continued from 1680 to this present time.* [ ]: [ ], 1712.

DORLING, E.E. 'Notes on the medieval heraldry remaining in the Cathedral church of Norwich', *Friends of the Cathedral Church of Norwich annual report* **4**, 1933, 8-24. Includes brief pedigree of Boleyn and Hoo, medieval.

EVANS, C.J. 'The heraldry of Norwich Cathedral', *N.A.* **8**, 1879, 57-86.

WILLIAMS, J.F. 'The brasses of Norwich Cathedral', *Transactions of the Monumental Brass Society* **9**, 1952-62, 366-74.

Dutch Church
KENT, ERNEST A. 'Notes on the Blackfriars Hall or Dutch Church, Norwich', *N.A.* **22**, 1926, 86-108. Includes monumental inscriptions.

'The Dutch church, Norwich', *East Anglian* **1**, 1864, 91-4. Monumental inscriptions.

Rosary Cemetery
HAMLIN, P.E. *Inscriptions in the Rosary Cemetery, Norwich.* Norfolk genealogy **18**, 1986. Monumental inscriptions, 1821-1986. Also includes the burial register, 1819-37, of this private, non-denominational cemetery.

St.Giles
EADE, SIR PETER. *Some account of the parish of St.Giles, Norwich, with maps, parish lists, and numerous illustrations.* Norwich: Jarrold & Sons, 1886. Includes an extensive list of monumental inscriptions; also list of ministers, directory for 1886, extracts from poll books, many biographies, rate lists, etc., etc.

St.Helen
LIDDLE, HARRY. 'Heraldry in St.Helen's Bishopsgate, Norwich', *Norfolk Standard* **3**(13), 1987, 164-5.

St.Margaret
WILLIAMS, J.F. 'The brasses of St.Margarets church, Norwich', *Transactions of the Monumental Brass Society* **9**, 1952-62, 118-25.

St.Michael at Coslaney
COMPTON, C.H. 'Notes on the church of St.Michael Coslaney, Norwich', *Journal of the British Archaeological Association* **42**, 1886, 395-9.

St.Stephen
MANNING, C.R. 'Notice of a monumental brass discovered under a pew in St.Stephens church, Norwich', *N.A.* **6**, 1864, 295-9. Includes full list of brasses in the church.

Old Buckenham
SINGH, F. DULEEP. 'Armorial glass in Old and New Buckenham churches', *N.A.* **15**, 1904, 324-34. See also **16**, 1907, 1.

B. *BY PLACE* continued
Ranworth
MORANT, A.W., & L'ESTRANGE, J. 'Notices of the
church at Randworth, Walsham Hundred', *N.A.*
7, 1872, 178-211. Includes monumental
inscriptions, list of rectors, etc.

Redenhall Deanery
'Church heraldry: Deanery of Redenhall, no.VI',
Eastern Counties Collecteana **1872-3**, 284-8.
See also Breckles Deanery

Sharrington
BLATCHLY, J.M. 'The brasses of Sharrington,
Norfolk', *Transactions of the Monumental
Brass Society* **12**(2), 1976, 159-68.

Stokesby
See Swafield

Swafield
'Copies of the inscriptions in the churches of
Swafield and Edingthorpe, and the churchyards
of Edingthorpe, Acle, Stokesby, & Hoveton
St.John', *N.A.M.* **2**, 1883, 509-23.

Thurlton
M., G.W. 'Monumental inscriptions at Thurlton,
Norfolk', *East Anglian* **1**, 1864, 151-2. See also
301.

Tunstead Hundred
RYE, WALTER. *The monumental inscriptions in the
Hundred of Tunstead in the county of Norfolk.*
Norwich: A. Goose, 1891.

Wells Next the Sea
RYE, WALTER. 'Wells church, Norfolk', *East
Anglian* **2**, 1866, 96-8. 40 monumental
inscriptions.

Wilton
GREEN, M.E.E. 'M.I's at St.James, Wilton, and
St.Peter's, Hockwold', *N.Anc.* **3**(5), 1984, 66.

Wiveton
LINNELL, C.L.S. 'Wiveton, Norfolk', *Transactions
of the Monumental Brass Society* **9**, 1952-62,
12-16. Includes folded pedigree of Brigge, 15-
17th c.

Wood Rising
STEER, FRANCIS W. *Woodrising church, Norfolk,
and notes on the Southwell and other families
connected with the parish.* [Woodrising]:
[Woodrising P.C.C.?], 1958. Includes memorial
inscriptions, with pedigrees of Southwell, 15-
17th c., and Bedell, 17-18th c.

Worstead
JEWSON, C.B. 'Memorial inscriptions, Worstead
meeting house', *N.Anc.* **1**(2), 1978, 25-7.
Transcribed in 1928.

C. *BY FAMILY*

Anguish
SMITH, M.Q. 'The monument of Thomas Anguish
in Saint George, Tombland, Norwich', *N.A.* **32**,
1961, 96-8. 1617.

Bernet
See Paston

Blennerhassett
'Ancient brass at Yelverton', *N.N.N.Q.* 2nd series,
1899-1904, 286-7. To Thomas Blennerhassett,
1590.

Brasyer
BADHAM, SALLY. 'Brasses to the Brasyer family in
St.Stephens church, Norwich', *Transactions of
the Monumental Brass Society* **12**, 1978, 295-
99.

Brooke
'Three quaint monumental inscriptions to
members of the Brooke family from
St.Swithin's Church, Norwich, *East Anglian*
N.S. **2**, 1887-8, 305-6.

Burroughes
DAVENEY, H. 'Mortuary inscriptions to the family
of Burroughes of Burlingham', *East Anglian* **1**,
1864, 360-61, 381 & 427-8.

Calthorpe
LINNELL, C.L.S. 'The Calthorpe brasses at
Antingham and Blakeney, Norfolk',
Transactions of the Monumental Brass Society
8, 1943-51, 264-9. Includes pedigree, 16th c.

Chamberlaine
SLEGG, W.B. 'The Chamberlaine tomb at East
Harling', *Transactions of the Monumental
Brass Society* **7**, 1934-42, 126-9. 15th c.

Cowall
See Ellingham

Crowmer
WORSHIP, FRANCIS. 'Crowmer monument,
Yarmouth church', *N.A.* **2**, 1849, 35-42.
Crowmer family.

C. BY FAMILY continued
De Burgh
MANNING, C.R. 'Monuments of the De Burgh and Ingoldsthorpe families in Burgh Green church, Cambridgeshire', *Archaeological journal* 34, 1877, 121-9. Includes pedigrees of De Burgh of Burgh Green, and of Ingoldsthorpe of Rainham, Norfolk; medieval.

Ellingham
GREENWOOD, J.R. 'Extracts from wills on gravestones at Fersfield and Stratton St.Michael, Norfolk', *Transactions of the Monumental Brass Society* 13, 1984, 381-6. Inscription to Jeffry Ellingham, 1493, and John Cowall, 1509.

Harvey
DAVENEY, H. 'The Harvey family of Norwich', *East Anglian* 1, 1864, 208-10, 241-2 & 266; 2, 1866, 140. Monumental inscriptions.

Hastings
HARTSHORNE, A. 'On the brass of Sir Hugh Hastings in Elsing church, Norfolk', *Archaeologia* 60, 1906, 25-42.
HOOPER, BARI, et al. 'The grave of Sir Hugh de Hastyngs, Elsing', *N.A.* 39, 1986, 88-99.

Heydon
LINNELL, C.L.S. 'Some notes on the brasses in Baconsthorpe church', *Transactions of the Monumental Brass Society* 8, 1943-51, 23-7. Heydon family brasses, 15-17th c.

Howard
MANNING, C.R. 'Brasses of Thomas Howard, second Duke of Norfolk, and Agnes, his wife', *N.A.* 8, 1879, 39-50. 16th c.
MARKS, R. 'The Howard tombs at Thetford and Framlingham: new discoveries', *Archaeological journal* 141, 1984, 252-68. Includes pedigree, 15-16th c.

Howman
FARROW, CHARLES. 'The Howman hatchment at Hockering', *Norfolk Standard* 2(11), 1981, 155-6. Also Lens family.

Ingoldsthorpe
See De Burgh

Jullys
GREENWOOD, J. ROGER. 'A brass fixed in the wrong Norfolk church', *N.A.* 37, 1980, 314-5. Commemorating William Jullys, 1486.

Lens
See Howman

Paston
FISKE, R.C. 'Sir William Paston's monument at North Walsham', *Norfolk heraldry* 1, 1991, 5-18. 1610; includes pedigree.
'The Paston and Bernet families', *East Anglian* 1, 1864, 183. Monumental inscriptions at Blofield, 17th c.

Peete
FISKE, R.C. 'St.Peter Hungate church, Norwich: a lost monument', *N.A.* 37, 1980, 325-6. Commemorating Richard Peete, 1802, and his family.

Scargill
LINNELL, C.L.S. 'The Scargill memorial, Mulbarton church, Norfolk', *Transactions of the Monumental Brass Society* 8, 1943-51, 91-3. 17th c.

Spelman
CLARK, H.O. 'A palimpsest brass at Narborough to John Spelman, esq., 1581', *N.A.* 25, 1935, 95-101.

Suckling
'The Suckling tomb in St.Andrews Church, Norwich', *N.N.N.Q.* 3rd series, 1904-5, 7-8. See also 16-20.

Thorp
PURCELL, DONOVAN. 'The de Thorp tomb, at Ashwellthorpe', *N.A.* 34, 1969, 253-8. Sir Edward de Thorp, c.1417.

Windham
KETTON-CREMER, R.W. 'A note on Thomas Windham', *N.A.* 32, 1961, 50-52. Monumental inscription, 1654.

10. HERALDRY

The standard work on Norfolk heraldry is:

FARRER, EDMUND. *The church heraldry of Norfolk: a description of all coats of arms on brasses, monuments, slabs, hatchments, etc., now to be found in the county.* 3 vols. Norwich: A.H. Goose, 1887-93.

See also:

CARTHEW, GEO. A. 'Extracts from a ms. diary of Peter Le Neve, esq. ... entitled Memorands in heraldry, of such entries as relate to the County of Norfolk', *N.A.* 2, 1849, 23-34, 111-26 & 369-91. Early 18th c. notes.

RYE, WALTER. *A list of coat armour used in Norfolk before the date of the first Herald's visitation of 1563.* 2 vols. Norwich: Roberts & Co., 1917. A separate index was published in 1918.

A number of rolls of arms have been described in print:

CARTHEW, G.A. 'Notice of a roll of arms belonging to Richard Charles Browne, esq.', *N.A.* 6, 1864, 73-102. Includes pedigree of Hastings, 12-16th c.

FARRER, EDMUND. 'A Norfolk armory of the 15th century', *N.A.M.* 3, 1887, 424-43.

LINNELL, C.L.S. 'A roll of arms of the Repps family', *N.A.* 33, 1965, 310-7. Includes pedigree of Repps, 17-19th c., and Jodrell, 18-20th c.

NORRIS, ANTHONY. *Three Norfolk armories: a transcript.* Norwich: A.H. Goose & Co., for Walter Rye, 1886.

For hatchments, see:

SUMMERS, PETER. *Hatchments in Britain, vol.2:* Norfolk and Suffolk. Phillimore, 1976.

TINDALE, J. 'Funeral hatchments in Norfolk', *East Anglian* 29, 1970, 278-80. Brief discussion.

For most works on monumental heraldry, see section 9 above. The following list includes grants and confirmations of arms, funeral certificates made by the Heralds, armorial bookplates, and a number of general studies.

Aldham

'Grants and confirmations of arms and crests', *M.G.H.* 5th series 8, 1932-4, 192-4. Grants to John Aldham of Shimpling, 1563, Steven Atkins of Norwich, 1576, and John Ayde of Lincolns Inn and Ketteringham, 1664.

Atkins

See Aldham

Ayde

See Aldham

Bagge

'Grants and confirmations of arms', *M.G.H.* 5th series 8, 1932-4, 221-3. Includes grants to William Bagge of Shipdham, 1656, Leonard Barrett of Defordham, Cambridgeshire, 1575, John Baspole of Beeston, 1576, and Richard Browne of Munsley, 1668.

Barrett

See Bagge

Baspole

See Bagge

Beloe

FARROW, C.W. 'The arms of the sexagenarian', *Norfolk Standard* 2(3), 1979, 40-41. Grant of arms to Beloe, 1805.

Boleyn

DENT, J.I. 'Boleyn heraldry in Norwich Cathedral', *Norfolk heraldry* 1, 1991, 29-34. Includes pedigree.

Browne

'Grants and confirmations of arms', *M.G.H.* 5th series 8, 1932-4, 247. Grants to Browne family, 1581, 1612 and 1632; and to John Cady of Great Ellingham, 1575.

See also Bagge

Cady

See Browne

Clippesby

See Linstead

Davie

FARROW, CHARLES. 'The Cufaude Davie papers', *Norfolk Standard* 3(3), 1982, 35-46. Davie family heraldry.

Elys

LAMBARDE, FANE. 'Elys of Norwich', *M.G.H.* 5th series 7, 1929-31, 153-4. Arms, 15th c.

Gilbert

FARROW, CHARLES. 'The arms of Gilbert of Norfolk', *Norfolk Standard* 3(2), 1982, 18-21.

'Grants and confirmations of arms and crests', *M.G.H.* 5th series 8, 1932-4, 310-14. Grantees includes Gilbert of North Burlingham, 1576, and Hacon, 1536.

FARROW, CHARLES. 'The arms of Gilbert of Norwich', *Norfolk Standard* 3(2), 1982, 18-21.

Gygges

'Grant of arms to Robert, Thomas and John Gygges, 1477, *M.G.H.* 3rd series 1, 1896, 1.

Hacon
See Gilbert

Heyward
'Grants and confirmations of arms and crests', *M.G.H.* 5th series **10**, 1938, 10-12. Includes grant to Heyward of Kerdeston, 1611.

Hougon
'Grants and confirmations of arms and crests', *M.G.H.* 5th series **8**, 1932-4, 338-41. Grants to Hougon of East Bradenham, 1546, Huby of Norwich, 1676, Humphrey of Suffolk, 1638, and Jenkinson of Tunstall, 1563.

Howman
'Grant of arms to Roger Howman, 1684', *M.G.H.* N.S. **1**, 1874, 397. Of Norwich.

Huby
See Hougon

Humphrey
See Hougon

Hunstone
R[YLANDS], J.P. 'Exemplification of arms and grant of crest to William Hunstone of Walpole, Co.Norfolk, by Sir Gilbert Dethick, knt., garter, 6 February, 1556-7', *M.G.H.* 4th series **5**, 1913, 1-2.

Huse
See Spany

Jenkinson
See Hougon

Le Strange
HURRELL, JOAN M.W. 'Some notes on the heraldry of the Le Strange family', *Norfolk Standard* **3**(6), 1983, 89-90.

Linstead
'Grants and confirmations of arms and crests', *M.G.H.* 5th series **9**, 1935-7, 15-17. Grants to Linstead, Mackerell and Clippesby families of Norfolk, and Mott of Essex, 16-18th c.

London
MARSHALL, GEORGE W. 'Arms of London, of Aldeby, Norfolk', *East Anglian* **3**, 1869, 8-9. Grant, 1664.

Long
HODSON, UNA LONG. 'The heraldry of Long of Dunstan and family connections', *Norfolk heraldry* **1**, 1991, 19-25. Reprinted from *Norfolk Standard* **2**(9), 1981, 120-25, & **2**(10), 1981, 137-9.

Mackerell
See Linstead

Maltby
'Grant of arms to Rev. Edward Maltby, D.D., 1829', *M.G.H.* 2nd series **1**, 1886, 81.

Millard
'Armorial bookplate: James Elwin Millard', *M.G.H.* N.S. **3**, 1880, 445-7. 18-19th c.

Mingaye
FETHERSTON, JOHN. 'Mingay: funeral certificate of John Mingaye, 1622', *M.G.H.* N.S. **1**, 1874, 17. Of Amringlale.

Mott
See Linstead

Palgrave
PALGRAVE, D.A. *Heraldry at North Barningham church.* Doncaster: Palgrave Society, 1976. Palgrave family.

Paston
'Friar Brackley's book of arms', *Ancestor* **10**, July 1904, 87-97. Mainly concerns the Paston family and their allies, 15th c.

Peake
See Rant

Pepys
LAMBARDE, FANE. 'Confirmations of arms and grants of crest to Thomas Pepys, 1563', *M.G.H.* 5th series **9**, 1935-7, 189.

Rant
'Grants and confirmations of arms and crests', *M.G.H.* 5th series **9**, 1935-7, 42-3. Includes grants to Rant of Norfolk, 1583, and Peake of Lincolnshire, 1583.

Salmon
'Grants and confirmations of arms and crests', *M.G.H.* 5th series **9**, 1935-7, 105-6. Grants to Salmon of West Barsham, 1591, and Shanke of Rollesby, 1561.

Shanke
See Salmon

Heraldry continued

Smithe
'Richard Smithe of Carleton Roade, 1622',
M.G.H. 2nd series **5**, 1894, 2. Funeral
certificate.

Spany
'Grants and confirmations of arms and crests',
M.G.H. 5th series **9**, 1935-7, 169-72. Includes
grants to Spany, 1563, Sybthorpe alias Huse of
Ludham, 1557, Tompson of Thorpe Market,
1602, etc.

Sybthorpe
See Spany

Tenison
TENISON, C.M. 'Tenisonia: grant of arms to Dr.
Philip Tenison, Archdeacon of Norfolk, 1660',
M.G.H. 3rd series **1**, 1896, 225-6.

Tompson
See Spany

Walpole
DENT, JOHN I. 'Heraldry at Mannington Hall',
Norfolk Standard **3**(7), 1984, 104-6 & 109.
Walpole family heraldry; includes pedigree, 18-
19th c.

FASSNIDGE, C.W. 'The tomb of the last Earl of
Orford at Wickmere', *Norfolk Standard* **2**(2),
1979, 21-5. Walpole family heraldry.

Windham
'Armorial bookplate: William Windham, esq.',
M.G.H. 2nd series **4**, 1892, 201. Of Felbrigg,
18th c.

Wodehouse
FISKE, R.C. 'The Wodehouse arms in heraldic glass
at Surrey House, Norwich', *Norfolk Standard*
1(3), 1976, 43-8.

Wood
'Funeral certificates: Robert Wood of Thurston,
1623', *M.G.H.* N.S. **4**, 1884, 178.

11. PROBATE RECORDS AND INQUISITIONS POST MORTEM

Indexes
Probate records—wills, inventories,
administration bonds, accounts, etc.—are
invaluable sources of genealogical information.
Wills in particular usually list all of the surviving
children, and often mention more distant kin,
together with places with which testators have
been associated. Most Norfolk wills were proved
either in the Consistory Court of the Diocese of
Norwich, or in the courts of the Archdeacons of
Norfolk and Norwich. Various other courts also
had probate jurisdiction. Published indexes of
wills are available for most of these courts; the
major exception is the Archdeaconry Court of
Norwich. Details of unpublished indexes are
given in Gibson's *Probate jurisdictions*, cf.
English genealogy: an introductory bibliography,
section 11.

Consistory Court
FARROW, M.A., ed. *Index to wills proved in the
Consistory Court of Norwich and now
preserved in the district probate registry at
Norwich, 1370-1550, and wills among the
Norwich enrolled deeds, 1286-1508*. Index
Library **69**, 1945. Also issued as N.R.S. **16**,
1944 (the title page of the latter gives 1298
instead of 1286).

FARROW, M.A. *Index to wills proved in the
Consistory Court of Norwich ... 1550-1603*.
N.R.S. **21**, 1950. Also published as Index
Library **73**.

FARROW, M.A., & BARTON, T.F., eds. *Index of wills
proved in the Consistory Court of Norwich and
now preserved in the District Probate Registry
at Norwich, 1604-1686*. N.R.S. **28**, 1958.

BARTON, THOMAS F., & FARROW, M.A., eds. *Index of
wills proved in the Consistory Court of
Norwich, 1687-1750, and now preserved in the
Norfolk and Norwich Record Office*. N.R.S. **34**,
1965.

BARTON, THOMAS F., FARROW, M.A., & BEDINGFELD,
A.L. *Index of wills proved in the Consistory
Court of Norwich, 1751-1818, and now
preserved in the Norfolk and Norwich Record
Office*. N.R.S. **38**, 1969.

FROSTICK, CLAIRE. *Index of wills proved in the
Consistory Court of Norwich, 1819-1857, and
now preserved in the Norfolk Record Office*.
N.R.S. **47**, 1980. Includes many Suffolk wills.

Norfolk Archdeaconry Court

PALGRAVE-MOORE, PATRICK. 'Index of wills proved in the Norfolk Archdeaconry Court, 1453-1542', *Norfolk genealogy* 3, 1971.

PALGRAVE-MOORE, PATRICK. 'Index of wills proved in the Norfolk Archdeaconry Court, 1542-1560', *Norfolk genealogy* 5, 1973.

PALGRAVE-MOORE, PATRICK. 'Index of wills proved in the Norfolk Archdeaconry Court, 1560-1603/4', *Norfolk genealogy* 10, 1978.

Peculiar Jurisdictions

NORFOLK RECORD OFFICE. 'Norfolk peculiar jurisdictions: index to probate records, 1416-1857', *Norfolk genealogy* 16, 1984, 1-65. See also 137-62 for index. Includes the Peculiars of the Dean and Chapter of Norwich (15 parishes throughout Norfolk), Great Cressingham, and of Castle Rising.

Prerogative Court of Canterbury

'Index of PCC wills deposited in the Society's library 1985', *N.Anc.* 4(4), 1986, 59. List of 55 will photocopies held by the N.N.G.S.

Innumerable other wills were also proved in the P.C.C. Many indexes and abstracts of these are available; full details are given in the companion volume to the present work, *English genealogy: an introductory bibliography*, section 11.

Abstracts

Many abstracts of Norfolk probate records have been printed. These include:

HARROD, HENRY. 'Extracts from early Norfolk wills', *N.A.* 1, 1847, 111-28 & 255-72. Wills, 1470-1522.

HARROD, HENRY. 'Extracts from early wills in the Norwich registries', *N.A.* 4, 1855, 317-39. See also 5, 1860, 209-20. Wills, 14-16th c., from the Diocesan court.

L'ESTRANGE, JOHN. 'Early Norfolk wills from the Norwich Registry', *N.A.M.* 1, 1877, 345-412. Abstracts of 14th c. wills.

'Old wills', *East Anglian* 1, 1864, 157-8. Brief abstracts, 14-16th c.

LEVINE, G. 'Some Norwich goldsmiths' wills', *N.A.* 35, 1973, 483-90. Abstracts of eight wills and two probate inventories, 1580-1645. A further six wills are abstracted in:

LEVINE, G.J. 'More Norwich goldsmiths' wills', *N.A.* 37, 1980, 208-212.

DASHWOOD, GEORGE HENRY, ed. 'Extracts from wills preserved in the muniment room at Stowe Bardolph', *N.A.* 2, 1849, 97-100. 14-16th c. wills.

CORNFORD, BARBARA. 'Inventories of the poor', *N.A.* 35, 1973, 118-125. Analysis, with a list of 15 inventories from Martham.

WILSON, J.H., ed. *Wymondham inventories, 1590-1641*. Creative history from East Anglia sources 1. Norwich: Centre for East Anglian Studies, 1983.

By Family

Barnes

'Catelyn of Kirby Cane, Norfolk', *East Anglian* N.S. 10, 1903-4, 376-8. Despite the title, the wills of James Barnes of Hales, 1675, and Bridget Barnes, 1677.

Browne

WILLIAMS, CHARLES. 'The will of Thomas Browne, mercer, Cheapside, London, father of Sir Thomas Browne of Norwich ...', *N.A.* 16, 1907, 132-46. 1613. Also includes will of Sir Thomas Browne of Norwich, 1679.

Calthorp

'Will of Sir William Calthorp, knight, 1494', *East Anglian* 2, 1865, 210-12.

Dusgate

S., F.H. 'Will of Francis Dusgate, 1632', *E.A.M.* 1910, 26-7.

Fairfax

'Fairfax wills of Norfolk and Suffolk', *Northern genealogist* 1, 1895, 49-53. Includes extracts from parish registers and marriage licences.

Fastolf

TURNER, DAWSON. 'Will of Sir John Fastolf, touching the establishment of his College at Caister', *N.A.* 2, 1849, 225-33. 1459.

Fox

'Wills of Christopher and John Fox, 1674 & 1675', *E.A.M.* 1929, 41-2.

Gallard

'Gallard wills', *M.G.H.* 2nd series 1, 1886, 157-9. Of Norfolk and Middlesex, 16-18th c.

Gooch

'Will of Dorothy Gooch, Great Yarmouth, 1776', *E.A.M.* 1908, 55-6.

Gotts

GOTTS, IAN. 'Some Norfolk names taken at will', *N.Anc.* 5(9), 1990, 208. Discusses will of Richard Gotts, 1594.

Grenegresse

'Old wills, no.IV: Thomas Grenegresse, of Pulham St.Mary Magdalen, Norfolk, 1503', *East Anglian* 2, 1866, 81.

Haste

BALL, H. HOUSTON. 'Will of Willyam Haste of Norwich, worsted weaver, A.D. 1539', *East Anglian* N.S. **10**, 1903-4, 103-5.

Hastings

CARTHEW, G.A. 'Extracts from the will of Martin Hastings, esq., 1574', *N.A.* **6**, 1864, 193-9.

Hatton

M., R.W. 'Will of Richard Hatton of Banningham, Norfolk, 1596', *E.A.M.* **1910**, 58-9.

Haultoft

JESSOPP, AUGUSTUS. 'Gilbert Haultoft's will', *N.A.* **8**, 1879, 177-82. 1457.

Irby

FOSTER, W.E. 'Wills of Irby family', *F.N.Q.* **5**, 1901-3, 8-12 & 40-43. Of Norfolk and Lincolnshire, 16-17th c.

Kirby

CURRER-BRIGGS, NOEL. *English adventurers and Virginian settlers: the co-ordinated use of seventeenth century British and American records by genealogists.* 3 vols. Phillimore, 1969. Abstracts of wills, 1484-1798, and legal proceedings, 1566-1700, relating to the Kirby and many allied families.

Le Grys

B., A. 'Will of Christopher Le Grys, of Billingford, 1601', *E.A.M.* **1920**, 94 & 97.

L'Estrange

MUSKETT, J.J., ed. 'Will of Sir Hamon L'Estrange of Hunstanton, 1654', *East Anglian* N.S. **1**, 1885-6, 153-5.

LE STRANGE, HAMON. 'Will of Sir Roger Le Strange, knt., A.D. 1505—21 Henry VII, from the archives at Hunstanton Hall', *N.A.* **9**, 1884, 226-39.

Lovell

'Will of Henry Lovell, Lord Morley', *M.G.H.* N.S. **1**, 1868, 61. Of Norfolk, Essex and Hertfordshire; 1489.

Mautby

See Paston

Parterich

'Will of Robert Parterich, of Gillingham, Norfolk, 1656', *E.A.M.* **1907**, 117-8.

Paston

TURNER, DAWSON. 'The will of Margaret Paston', *N.A.* **3**, 1852, 157-76. 1481. Includes pedigree of Mautby.

Payne

CULLUM, G. MILNER GIBSON. 'The family of Payne of Norfolk: abstracts of wills at Norwich', *East Anglian* N.S. **11**, 1905-6, 129-31, 146-9, 172-3, 177-9, 206-7, 216-7 & 236-7.

Peterson

MANNING, C.R. 'The will and codicil of Peter Peterson, citizen and goldsmith of Norwich, 1603', *N.A.* **11**, 1892, 259-302. Includes pedigree, 15-17th c.

Salter

GREENWOOD, J. ROGER. 'The will of Thomas Salter of London, 1558', *N.A.* **38**, 1983, 280-95. Salter came from a Norfolk family.

Seffrey

RYE, WALTER. 'A bondsman's will and property', *East Anglian* N.S. **3**, 1889-90, 377-8. Thomas Seffrey of Kenninghall, 1541.

Skayman

'Will of Robert Skayman (1505)', *E.A.M.* **1909**, 43. Of North Creake.

Smyth

RUTLEDGE, P. 'The goods of William Smyth', *Yarmouth Archaeology* **2**(2), 1985, 51-5. Probate inventory, 1580.

Starling

ENGLAND, MICHAEL. 'John Starling of Hockering, gent.', *N.Anc.* **3**(3), 1983, 27. Will, 1757.

Tanner

MUSKETT, J.J. 'A Norwich bishop of the eighteenth century', *East Anglian* N.S. **13**, 1909-10, 17-21. Will of Thomas Tanner, Bishop of Norwich, 1733.

Tusser

CLARK, C., ed. *The last will and testament of Thomas Tusser ... to which is added his metrical autobiography, &c.* Great Totham: C. Clark, 1846. 1580.

Ward

'Abstract of will of Susannah Ward, late of North Walsham, Co.Norfolk', *East Anglian* N.S. **3**, 1889-90, 379. 1775. Also of Battersea, Surrey.

Wells

S., S. 'Will of Amy Wells of New Buckenham, 1766', *E.A.M.* **1926**, 25-6.

'Will of John Welles of Warham, Norfolk, 1749', *E.A.M.* **1926**, 21.

West

BOLINGBROKE, LEONARD G. 'Two Elizabethan inventories', *N.A.* **15**, 1904, 91-108. Inventories of John West, 1513, and Sir Roger Wodehouse, 1588.

Wodehouse

See West

Yates

'The will of John Yates, 1657', *E.A.M.* **1934**, 18-19 & 23-4.

Inquisitions Post Mortem

Inquisitions post mortem are invaluable sources of genealogical information, and are particularly useful in tracing the descent of manors prior to 1646. They were taken on the deaths of tenants in chief, and recorded lands held, with the names and ages of heirs. For Norfolk inquisitions, see:
'Inquisitions post mortem or escheats', in SELBY, WALFORD D., ed. *Norfolk records* **1**. Norwich: Agas H. Goose & Co., 1886, 1-92. For 1485-1646. Continued by:
RYE, WALTER, ed. *Norfolk records, [2]: being an index to four series of Norfolk inquisitions.* Norwich: Norfolk & Norwich Archaeological Society, 1892.

12. OFFICIAL LISTS OF NAMES

Governments are keen on listing their subjects—a trait for which genealogists have cause to be thankful, since the lists which result enable us to locate our ancestors precisely in time and place. Official lists have been compiled for a multitude of reasons—taxation, defence, voting, land ownership, etc.

Domesday book provides the earliest general listing of manorial lords, and has recently been republished:
BROWN, PHILIPPA, ed. *Domesday Book, 33: Norfolk.* 2 vols. Chichester: Phillimore, 1983. An earlier edition is printed in the *Victoria County History* (see above, section 1).

Taxation Lists

The 'aid' of 1346 is the earliest Norfolk tax list to have been printed; it enables us to easily identify the chief tenants of the crown:
TYSSEN, JOHN R. DANIEL, ed. 'Extracts from the *Liber Niger Scaccarii* and the account of the aid taken 20th Edward III', *N.A.M.* **1**, 1877, 1-106.

The poll tax is not a modern invention—far from it. Merton poll-tax payers for 1327 and 1381 are listed in:
GREY, RICHARD DE. 'The Black Death and the Peasants Revolt', *N.Anc.* **1**(6), 1979, 78-9.

The crown's major source of tax revenue in the late medieval and early modern period was the subsidy. Subsidy returns survive in bulk; however, only a few have been printed. These include:
DASHWOOD, G.H. 'Remarks on a subsidy roll in the possession of the Corporation of Lynn Regis', *N.A.* **1**, 1847, 334-54. Probably of 1329 for Kings Lynn.
HUDSON, WILLIAM. 'Norwich and Yarmouth in 1332: their comparative prosperity', *N.A.* **16**, 1917, 177-96. Includes full transcript of subsidy rolls.
RYE, WALTER. 'Notes on the port and trade of Cromer alias Shipden', *N.A.* **7**, 1872, 276-88. Includes subsidy roll, 1332, etc.
VIRGOE, ROGER. 'A Norwich taxation list of 1451', *N.A.* **40**, 1989, 145-54. Subsidy return, with brief biographical notes.
'Norfolk subsidy roll, 15 Henry VIII'. *N.A.M.* **2**, 1883, 399-410. 1523.
MILLICAN, PERCY, ed. 'Lay subsidy, 1581: assessor's certificates for the Norfolk hundreds of Depwade, South Greenhoe, Henstead, Mitford and Shropham', *N.R.S.* **17**, 1944, 93-127.

HUDSON, WILLIAM. 'Assessment of the Hundred of Forehoe, Norfolk, in 1621: a sidelight on the difficulties of national taxation', *N.A.* **2**, 1923, 285-309. Transcript.

Two returns from 'voluntary' levies of the mid-seventeenth century are in print:

BEECHENO, F.R. 'The Norwich subscription for the regaining of Newcastle, 1643', *N.A.* **18**, 1914, 149-60.

WILLIAMS, P.M., ed. 'Norwich subscriptions to the voluntary gift of 1662', *N.R.S.* **1**, 1931, 69-86.

After the restoration of 1662, the subsidy gave way to the hearth tax. The returns of 1664 and 1666 have been published in full, providing us with reasonably complete lists of heads of households at those dates. All Norfolk genealogists should check:

FRANKEL, M.S., & SEAMAN, P.J., eds. *Norfolk hearth tax assessment, Michaelmas 1664. Norfolk genealogy* **15**, [1983?].

SEAMAN, P. *Norfolk and Norwich hearth tax assessment: Lady Day 1666.* Norfolk genealogy **20**, 1988.

Many other hearth tax records remain unpublished. A guide to them is provided by:

SEAMAN, PETER. 'A guide to the Norfolk hearth tax records in the Public Record Office, London', *N.Anc.* **2**(2), 1980, 23-7; 2(3), 1980, 30-34; 2(5), 1981, 58-61; 2(6), 1981, 73-7, & 2(9), 1982, 122-6.

The unpopularity of the hearth tax led to its abandonment, and to a search for alternatives. One such alternative was the window tax: the return for Thurning in 1696 is printed in:

PALGRAVE-MOORE, PATRICK. 'The Norfolk window tax', *N.Anc.* **3**(6), 1984, 82.

Muster Rolls

Muster rolls offer another potential source of information. All adult males were obliged to bear arms in the defence of the realm, and to appear at musters, where their names were entered on a roll. A number of these rolls and other associated documents have been published:

HUDSON, WILLIAM. 'Norwich militia in the fourteenth century', *N.A.* **14**, 1901, 263-320.

Extracts from original manuscripts belonging to the Norwich Corporation, and other documents. Norwich: Norfolk and Norwich Archaeological Society, 1846. Also published as *N.A.* **1**, 1847, 1-40. Extracts from papers concerned mainly with musters, 16th c.

Muster Rolls continued

COZENS-HARDY, B. 'A muster roll and clergy list in the hundred of Holt, circa 1523', *N.A.* **22**, 1926, 45-58. Lists both clergy and laity.

DALE, MARIAN, ed. *Muster roll for the Hundred of North Greenhoe, circa 1523.* N.R.S. **1**, 1931, 41-68.

BRADFER-LAWRENCE, H.L., ed. *The musters returns for divers hundreds in the county of Norfolk, 1569, 1572, 1574 and 1577.* 2 vols. N.R.S. **6-7**, 1936. Primarily the muster return for fifteen hundreds in 1577, plus supplementary material for other musters.

EDWARDS, STANLEY, ed. 'Musters at Lynn in 1573', *N.A.M.* **1**, 1877, 199-203. Lists those appearing at Kings Lynn.

RYE, WALTER, ed. *State papers relating to musters, beacons, shipmoney, &c., in Norfolk, from 1626 chiefly to the beginning of the Civil War.* Norwich: Norfolk and Norwich Archaeological Society, 1907. Includes many names, although not a full muster roll for the county.

DUNN, RICHARD MINTA, ed. *Norfolk lieutenancy journal, 1660-1676.* N.R.S. **45**, 1977. Includes appendix of 'lieutenancy biographies'.

COZENS-HARDY, B., ed. *Norfolk lieutenancy journal, 1676-1701.* N.R.S. **30**, 1961. Gives many names of those liable to serve.

TOOKE, DEREK. 'Muster roll: East and West Flegg, 16th January 1683-4', *N.Anc.* **3**(9), 1985, 124-6.

Loyalty Oaths

The question of allegiance was the major issue of the Civil War. To whom was loyalty due—the King, or Parliament? In 1641/2, an oath of loyalty—the Protestation—was demanded from the populace; surviving returns give the signatures of almost all adult males. For Norfolk, unfortunately, only one return has been published:

B[LAGG], T.M. 'Protestation oath at East Rudham, 1641-2', in ASTLEY, H.J. DUKINFIELD, ed. *N.P.R.M.* **8**, *P.P.R.S.* **202**, 1914, 151-3.

Poll Books

During the 18th and 19th centuries, Parliamentary elections were not secret, and many poll books listing electors and how they cast their votes were published. One of them has been re-printed in:

CAMPLING, ARTHUR, ed. 'Elections for two knights of the shire for Norfolk, 1702: votes polled for Sir Edward Ward, Bart.', N.R.S. **8**, 1936, 41-70.

Other poll books may be identified in Darroch and Taylor's *Bibliography of Norfolk* (above, section 1), and in the works listed in section 12D of *English genealogy: an introductory bibliography*, the companion volume to the present work.

The Census

Much the most useful lists, for the genealogist, are those deriving from the nineteenth-century censuses. For Norfolk, many indexes and extracts have been published; they are listed here by date and place:

1841

FINNETT, JANET. 'Index of surnames from various Norfolk parishes taken from the 1841 census returns', *N.Anc.* **3**(7), 1984, 97-8. Covers Booton, Colby, Hautbois Magna, Mannington, Oulton, Culton workhouse, Saxthorpe, Skeyton, Tuttington, Wickmere and Wolterton.

1851

JONES, H. 'Index of surnames from various Norfolk parishes, 1851 census', *N.Anc.* **4**(5), 1986, 72-4. Includes Antingham, Baconsthorpe, Barningham Winter, Bodham, Edgefield, Gimmingham, Glandford, Bayfield, Gunton, Thorpe Market, Hanworth, Hempstead by Holt, Hunworth, Kelling, and Knapton.

JONES, HONOR. '1851 census of Aylsham/West Beckham Union houses', *N.Anc.* **3**(2), 1983, 25. Mainly surnames only.

SIMONS, JANICE. '1851 census indexes', *N.Anc.* **5**(3), 1988, 56-7. For Grimstone, South Lynn, and Tilney St.Lawrence.

Norwich

PAGE, R., & PALGRAVE-MOORE, PATRICK, eds. *Census of Norwich, 1851.* Norfolk genealogy 7 & 9, 1975-7. Pt.1. St.Martin at Palace, St.Martin at Oak. Pt.2. St.Helen, Ss.Simon and Jude, St.Michael at Plea, St.Etheldred, St.Peter Hungate, St.Edmund, St.James. Continued in:

PAGE, R., ed. *Census of Norwich, 1851: parish or township of St.George Colgate.* Norwich: N.N.G.S., 1983.

WATKINS, BERYL, ed. *Census of Norwich, 1851: parish of St.John de Sepulchre.* Norwich: N.N.G.S., 1985.

BANKOWSKY, HEATHER, ed. *Census of Norwich, 1851: parish of St.Lawrence.* Norwich: N.N.G.S., 1985.

BANKOWSKY, HEATHER, ed. *Census of Norwich, 1851: parish of St.Margaret.* Norwich: N.N.G.S., 1987.

BANKOWSKY, H., ed. *Census of Norwich, 1851: parish or township of St.Michael at Thorn.* Norwich: N.N.G.S., 1984.

BANKOWSKY, HEATHER, ed. *Census of Norwich, 1851: parish or township of St.Swithin.* Norwich: N.N.G.S., 1984.

Hull and Kensington

EDMONDS, JENNIFER A. *Born in Norfolk or Suffolk: a collection of 1851 census strays from Kensington and Hull.* [The author], [1989].

London

Norfolk & Suffolk strays in the 1851 London census. Norwich: Worldwide Family History Services, 1992. Vol.1: Kensington. Vol.2: Westminster. Vol.3: St.George's, Hanover Sq.

1871

Jarrow and South Shields

ROUNCE, W.E. 'An extract of the names of Norfolk people living in Jarrow and South Shields from the 1871 census', *N.Anc.* **3**(1), 1983, 8-12.

Winchester

LAST, C.F. 'Norfolk strays, 1871/1881 census', *N.Anc.* **5**(4), 1989, 81. In Winchester, Hampshire.

1881

The Mormons are currently preparing a microfiche index to the 1881 census, which will be an essential tool for every genealogist. See also:

Colwich

WOOD, MARJORIE E. 'Norfolk strays, 1881 census', *N.Anc.* **5**(2), 1988, 39. Mainly from Colwich, Staffordshire.

New Windsor

CULLINGHAM, GORDON. 'Strays: 1881 census of New Windsor: extracts of persons from Suffolk/Norfolk', *Suffolk roots* **8**(4), 1982, 78-9; **9**(1), 1983, 9-10; **9**(2), 37-9.

Tower of London

EDMONDS, JENIFER. 'Norfolk strays, 1881 census', *N.Anc.* **5**(9), 1990, 227. Mainly from the Tower of London.

Wandsworth

EDMONDS, JENIFER. 'Norfolk strays: 1881 census', *N.Anc.* **5**(2), 1988, 38. From Wandsworth, Surrey.

Woolwich

BONWELL, LES. 'Norfolk strays from Woolwich census, 1881: district of Holy Trinity, Kent', *N.Anc.* **4**(5), 1986, 78.

Landowners

A different census was taken in 1873: everyone who owned an acre or more of land was listed. The returns for Norfolk have been recently reprinted:

The 1873 return of owners of land in Norfolk. Norwich: Palgrave-Moore & Co., 1990. This return is also available in the *Parliamentary papers.*

13. DIRECTORIES AND MAPS

Directories are an invaluable source for locating people in the past. For the nineteenth century, they are the equivalent of the modern phone book. Many directories for Norfolk were published. The list which follows is selective; others may be identified in Darroch and Taylor's *Bibliography of Norfolk*, and in the volumes listed in section 13 of *English genealogy: an introductory bibliography*. Arrangement here is by date and place.

WHITE, WILLIAM. *History, gazetteer and directory of Norfolk and the City and County of the City of Norwich* ... Sheffield: W. White, 1836-90. 5 issues.

Kelly's directory of Norfolk. Kelly & Co., 1846-1937. 22 issues. Title varies; sometimes referred to as *Post Office directory* ... and issued in one volume with various other counties.

Slater's (late Pigot & Co.) Royal national and commercial directory of the counties of Bedfordshire, Cambridgeshire, Huntingdonshire, Lincolnshire, Norfolk, Northampton and Suffolk ... Manchester: I. Slater, 1850.

Hunt & Co's directory of East Norfolk, with part of Suffolk, comprising comprehensive lists of the commercial and private residents in the City of Norwich, the sea ports and watering places of Yarmouth and Lowestoft, Cromer and Mundesley, the inland towns of Attleburgh, Aylsham, Beccles, Buckenham, Bungay, Diss, East Dereham, East Harling, Foulsham, Harleston, Hingham, Holt, Loddon, North Walsham, Reepham, and Wymondham, and in 166 of the circumjacent villages ... E.Hunt & Co., 1850.

WHITE, FRANCIS & CO. *History, gazetteer and directory of Norfolk and the City and County of the City of Norwich* ... Sheffield: Francis White & Co., 1854.

Craven and Co's commercial directory of the County of Norfolk containing an alphabetical list of the nobility, gentry, merchants, professions, trades, etc. ... Nottingham: Craven & Co., 1856.

Melville's directory and gazetteer of Norwich, Yarmouth, Dereham, Swaffham ... Ipswich, Bury St.Edmunds, Woodbridge ... Norwich: F.R. Melville & Co., 1856.

J.G. Harrod & Co's postal and commercial directory of Norfolk and Norwich, including Lowestoft in the County of Suffolk, containing a brief descriptive account of the towns, parishes and villages, followed by a directory. J.G. Harrod & Co., 1863-79. 5 issues.

Simpson's Norwich directory and court guide including Aylsham and Wymondham and surrounding villages ... Simpson & Co., 1864.

Deacon's Cambridgeshire, Norfolk and Suffolk court guide and county blue book: a fashionable record, professional register and general survey of the counties ... Charles William Deacon & Co., 1883-93.

Cromer

Jarrold's directory of Cromer and neighbourhood, containing street directory, alphabetical lists of inhabitants, and professional and trade directory. Jarrold & Sons, 1889.

The Cromer almanack and directory. Holt: Rounce & Wortley, 1929-30. 2 issues.

Dereham

F.W. Count's illustrated Dereham almanack for 1904 ... East Dereham: F.W. Count, 1904.

Great Yarmouth

Cobb's directory of the borough of Great Yarmouth in the County of Norfolk, with Southtown and Gorleston in Suffolk. Great Yarmouth: W. Cobb & Co., 1863.

Mathieson's Yarmouth and Lowestoft directory for 1867-68. Yarmouth: G. Nall, 1867.

Morris & Co's commercial directory and gazetteer of Suffolk with Great Yarmouth and Newmarket. Nottingham: Morris & Co., 1868. Newmarket, Cambridgeshire.

Godfrey's directory of the borough of Great Yarmouth ... with Southtown and Gorleston. Great Yarmouth: C.W. Godfrey, 1874. Continued by: *Steer's commercial and general directory of the town and borough of Great Yarmouth* ... Great Yarmouth: C. Steer, 1878.

Great Yarmouth, Gorleston and Southtown directory ... Hull: W.J. Cook & Co., Great Yarmouth: Jarrold & Sons, 1886-1901. 4 eds.

Kelly's directory of Great Yarmouth, Gorlestone and Southtown. Kellys, 1900-1972. 32 issues.

Kings Lynn

Directory of King's Lynn in the County of Norfolk for 1846. Whittaker and Co., [1846].

Kelly's directory of Kings Lynn and neighbourhood. Kelly's Directories, 1928-74. 20 issues.

Norwich

The Norwich directory, or gentleman and tradesmen's assistant, containing an alphabetical list of the principal inhabitants, their address, occupation and residence ... Norwich: W. Chase & Co., 1783-4. 2 issues. The 1783 edition reprinted Kings Lynn: Michael Winton, 1991.

PECK, THOMAS. *The Norwich directory, containing an alphabetical list of the principal inhabitants, their address, profession or trade ...* Norwich: J. Payne, [1802].

A concise history & directory of ... Norwich for 1811 ... Norwich: C. Berry, jun., 1810.

BLYTH, G.K. *The Norwich guide and directory ...* R. Hastings, 1842. Includes many historical notes, as well as a directory.

Rogers directory of Norwich and neighbourhood. Norwich: Jarrold & Sons, 1859.

Mathieson's Norwich directory for 1867. Norwich: Fletcher & Son, 1867.

Colman's directory of Norwich. Norwich: J.A. Colman & T.B. Fuller, 1877.

BANE, JAMES J. *The Imperial Postal directory of the City and County of Norwich, including the names of the principal private residents of the village of Thorpe, in the County of Norfolk, and a business directory of Yarmouth and Lowestoft; also an abbreviated gazetteer of the County of Norfolk, with a list of every town village and hamlet in the counties of Suffolk, Cambridgeshire and Essex, with their post towns.* Norwich: J.J. Hamilton & Co., 1879.

Post Office Norwich district directory. Eyre Brothers, 1883.

Directory of the city of Norwich including its hamlets. Jarrold & Sons, 1887-1922. 11 issues. Title varies; sometimes *Jarrold's Norwich directory.*

Norwich and District trades directory. Edinburgh: Town and County Directories, 1901-32. 14 issues; title varies.

City of Norwich business directory. Norwich: Pioneer Printing, 1902.

The new directory of Norwich. Norwich: Goose & Son, 1914.

Kelly's directory of the city of Norwich. Kelly's Directories, 1924-75. 29 editions.

Sheringham

Rounce & Wortley's Sheringham almanack including alphabetical directory of householders. Holt: Rounce & Wortley, 1933.

Thetford

The Thetford household almanack and directory. Thetford: F. Lucy, 1869-74. Publisher varied.

Thetford and District almanac. Thetford: H. Green, 1929-37. 3 issues.

Maps

In addition to directories, the genealogist also needs maps—and especially historic maps—to identify the places mentioned in his sources. Of particular value are the first edition 1" Ordnance Survey maps; these were made accurately, at a date before the modern landscape became afflicted with the concrete jungle of modern suburbia. A convenient modern edition is provided by:

The Old Series Ordnance Survey maps of England and Wales ... Volume 5: Lincolnshire, Rutland and East Anglia. Lympne Castle: Harry Margary, 1987. Reprinted sheet maps from the original 1" survey are also available from the publishers David & Charles.

An older map of the county has been reproduced in:

Faden's map of Norfolk. N.R.S. **42**, 1973. Six sheets in slip case, originally published 1797.

For Norwich, see:

LOBEL, M.D., ed. *The atlas of historic towns, vol.2: Bristol, Cambridge, Coventry, Norwich.* Scolar Press, 1975.

Many other maps are listed in:

CHUBB, T. *A descriptive list of the printed maps of Norfolk, 1574-1916, with biographical notes and a tabular index.* Norwich: Jarrold & Sons, 1928. Also includes STEPHEN, GEO. A. *A descriptive list of Norwich plans, 1541-1914.*

The essential guide to locating place-names is:

FONE, JOHN. *Norfolk gazetteer with administrative areas.* Norwich: N.N.G.S., 1989. Originally published in *N.Anc.* 1982-6, passim. Unfortunately, this only gives parishes and the larger hamlets. If the place-name you want to check is not mentioned, you may need to check the as yet incomplete English Place Name Society's volume:

SANDRED, KARL INGE, & LINDSTROM, BENGT. *The place-names of Norfolk, pt.1: the place-names of the City of Norwich.* English Place-Name Society **61**, 1989.

Reference may also be made to the much less detailed:

RYE, JAMES. *A popular guide to Norfolk place-names.* Dereham: Lanks Press, 1991.

RYE, WALTER. 'An index to the names of the chief places (not being towns or villages) occuring on the Ordnance map of Norfolk and in Bryant's map of Norfolk', *N.A.M.* **2**, 1883, 305-19.

Every Norfolk genealogist should obtain a copy of the parish map published by the Institute of Heraldic and Genealogical Studies.

Dialect

Dialect words may also cause you problem. To solve them, a number of dialect glossaries are available:

FORBY, ROBERT. *The vocabulary of East Anglia.* 2 vols. Newton Abbot: David & Charles, 1970. Originally published J.B. Nichols & Son, 1830.

RYE, WALTER. 'The vocabulary of East Anglia', *N.A.M.* **3**, 1887, 465-602. Glossary.

RYE, WALTER. *Glossary of words used in East Anglia, founded on that of Forby.* English Dialect Society, 1895.

14. ECCLESIASTICAL RECORDS

Church records are of the greatest importance to genealogists. This reflects the fact that ecclesiastical involvement in the life of society was formerly much wider than it is today. Some ecclesiastical records, i.e. parish registers, probate records and churchwardens' accounts, are dealt with in other sections of this book. This chapter focuses on those records which are more directly concerned with ecclesiastical administration.

An outline of the history of the Diocese is provided by:

JESSOPP, AUGUSTUS. *Norwich.* Diocesan histories. S.P.C.K., 1884.

There are a number of works devoted to the general history of the Diocese. The following list is arranged in rough chronological order:

HARPER-BILL, CHRISTOPHER, ed. *English episcopal acta, VI: Norwich, 1070-1214.* Oxford: O.U.P., 1990. Includes many deeds.

LANDON, L. 'Early archdeacons of Norwich Diocese', *Suffolk Institute of Archaeology proceedings* **20**, 1930, 11-35.

HOWLETT, RICHARD. 'Early parochial clergy in Norfolk not mentioned by Blomefield', *N.A.M.* **2**, 1883, 427-33. Medieval; supplements Blomefield's *History* (see section 1 above).

CATTERMOLE, PAUL & COTTON, SIMON. 'Medieval church building in Norfolk', *N.A.* **38**, 1983, 235-79. Includes a gazetteer, noting the names of many benefactors.

LE NEVE, JOHN. *Fasti ecclesiae Anglicanae, 1300-1541. IV: Monastic Cathedrals (Southern Province).* comp. B. Jones. Athlone Press, 1963.

TANNER, NORMAN P. *The church in late medieval Norwich, 1370-1532.* Toronto: Pontifical Institute of Medieval Studies, 1984. A detailed study, with appendices including much information on probate records, and a transcript of Bishop Goldwell's visitation of Norwich in 1492.

TANNER, NORMAN P., ed. *Heresy trials in the Diocese of Norwich, 1428-31.* Camden 4th series **20**, Royal Historical Society, 1977. Records 55 trials.

JESSOPP, A., ed. *Visitations of the Diocese of Norwich, A.D. 1492-1532.* Camden Society, N.S. **43**, 1888. Record of ecclesiastical visitations; many names of religious.

STONE, E.D., ed. *Norwich Consistory Court depositions, 1499-1512 and 1518-1530.* rev. B. Cozens-Hall. N.R.S. **10**, 1938. Includes names of many plaintiffs, defendants and witnesses.

Ecclesiastical Records *continued*

HOULBROOKE, R.A. 'Persecution of heresy and protestantism in the Diocese of Norwich under Henry VIII', *N.A.* **35**, 1973, 308-26. Includes list of the persecuted, 1499-1547.

SPURGIN, JOHN. *The Norfolk and Norwich martyrs who suffered in the reigns of Henry VIII and Queen Mary.* Norwich: Charles Muskett, 1855.

LINNELL, CHARLES LAWRENCE SCRUTON. *Some East Anglian clergy.* Fath Press, 1961. General discussion, 16-19th c.

BASKERVILLE, G. 'Married clergy and pensioned religious in the Norwich Diocese, 1555', *English Historical Review* **48**, 1933, 43-64 & 199-228. Many names of clergy.

HOULBROOKE, R.A., ed. *The letter book of John Parkhurst, Bishop of Norwich, compiled during the years 1571-5.* N.R.S. **43**, 1975.

SAUNDERS, H.W. 'A list of the clergy of Norfolk and their status: 35 Elizabeth 1592-3', *N.A.* **18**, 1914, 78-104. Gives names, parishes, degrees, etc.

WILLIAMS, J.F., ed. *Diocese of Norwich: Bishop Redman's visitation, 1597: presentments in the Archdeaconries of Norwich, Norfolk, and Suffolk.* N.R.S. **18**, 1946. Gives names of many clergy, churchwardens, etc.

JESSOPP, AUGUSTUS. 'The condition of the Archdeaconry of Norwich in 1603', *N.A.* **10**, 1888, 1-49 & 166-84. Gives names of clergy and patrons.

BARTON, THOMAS F., ed. *The registrum vagum of Anthony Harison.* 2 vols. N.R.S. **32-3**, 1963-4. Includes lists of the Diocesan clergy 1605, of ordinands and institutions, of excommunicants and recusants, clergy muster roll, 1608, and many other records of diocesan administration.

CARTER, E.H. *The Norwich subscription books: a study of the subscription books of the Diocese of Norwich, 1637-1800.* T. Nelson & Son, [1937]. General discussion of an important source for the clergy; includes many names.

HOOD, MRS. IVO (CHRISTOBEL M.) *Sequestered loyalists and Bartholomew sufferers, and other historical papers.* Jarrolds, 1922. Biographical notes on clergy ejected during the Commonwealth and Restoration.

GRIGSON, FRANCIS. 'East Anglian institutions to benefices', *East Anglian* N.S. **1**, 1885-6, 71-2, 89-91 & 105-7. For Cambridgeshire, Essex, Norfolk and Suffolk, by the Vicar General, or the Archbishop, of Canterbury, 1660-1838.

CARTER, E.H. *Norfolk incumbents for the period 1660-1720, being addenda and corrigenda to Blomefield's History of Norfolk and Bryant's Norfolk churches, abstracted from the subscription books of the Diocese of Norwich.* Norwich: H.W. Hunt, 1936. Listed by Hundred and parish; supplements Blomefield's *History* (see above, section 1).

TURNER, DAWSON. *List of Norfolk beneficies, with the names of their respective incumbents and patrons, and the date of their several presentations ... continued from Blomefield's History of Norfolk to the present time.* Norwich: Charles Muskett, 1847.

The Norwich Diocesan calendar and clergy list ... Norwich: Cundall and Miller, 1859-1948. Continued as *Norwich Diocesan directory and clergy list ...*, 1949-. Lists clergy.

A number of works provide information on the personnel of the church in particular places. They are listed here by parish:

Attleborough

BARRETT, JONATHAN T. *Memorials of the parochial church, the collegiate chantry, and the chapel of St.Mary, commonly called Mortimers Chapel, in the parish of Attleborough, in the County of Norfolk ...* John W. Parker, 1848. Includes pedigrees of the church's founders and patrons, with some memorial inscriptions, and a list of rectors and patrons.

Great Yarmouth

PALMER, C.F.R. *The friar-preachers, or blackfriars, of Great Yarmouth, Norfolk',* Reliquary N.S. **1**, 1897, 139-46. Includes obits of religious, benefactors, etc.

Kings Lynn

LITTLE, A.G., & STONE, E., eds. 'Corrodies of the Carmelite friary of Lynn', *Journal of Ecclesiastical History* **9**, 1958, 8-29. 14-15th c. Corrodies were grants of free board and lodging, usually in return for services.

PALMER, C.F.R. 'The friar-preachers, or blackfriars, of Kings Lynn', *Archaeological Journal* **41**, 1884, 79-86. Includes lists of benefactors and notes on individual friars.

Norwich

RYE, WALTER. 'The riot between the monks and citizens of Norwich in 1272', *N.A.M.* **2**, 1883, 17-89. Includes a list of rioters, and many documentary abstracts.

Norwich *continued*

PALMER, C.F.R. 'The friar-preachers, or blackfriars, of Norwich', *Reliquary* N.S. **2**, 1888, 161-70 & 210-14; **3**, 1889, 42-9 & 98-108. Includes names of priors, notes on benefactors, obits, etc.

Cathedral

WILLIAMS, J.F., & COZENS-HARDY, B., eds. *Extracts from the two earliest minute books of the Dean and Chapter of Norwich Cathedral, 1566-1649.* N.R.S. **24**, 1953. Includes lists of clergy and officials, etc.

St.Stephen

'St.Stephens parish, Norwich: list of incumbents', *East Anglian* N.S. **10**, 1903-4, 57.

Thetford

PALMER, C.F.R. 'The friar-preachers, or blackfriars, of Thetford', *Reliquary* N.S. **1**, 1887, 196-204. Includes obits of religious, benefactors, etc.

Weston Longville

WOODFORDE, JAMES. *The diary of a country parson.* ed. John Beresford. 5 vols. Oxford University Press, 1924-31. 18th c. Partly written at Weston Longville. Reviewed in:

HORTH, R.A. 'I took a little rhubarb instead of the pill', *N.Anc.* **2**(12), 1983, 158-60. Includes list of surnames mentioned.

Nonconformists

Whilst the records of the Church of England are voluminous in extent, genealogists must not neglect nonconformist records. For an early listing of Norfolk and Suffolk nonconformists, see:

JEWSON, C.B. 'Return of conventicles in Norwich Diocese, 1669: Lambeth ms. no.639', *N.A.* **33**, 1965, 6-34.

Baptists

PALGRAVE-MOORE, PATRICK. 'Norfolk Baptists and their records', *N.Anc.* **3**(3), 1983, 39-41. General discussion and summary list of records.

JEWSON, CHARLES B., ed. 'The account book of the *Baptised* church in the City of Norwich, 1726-1745', N.R.S. **22**, 1951, 41-64. Includes lists of members, etc.

JEWSON, C.B. 'Historic documents of St.Mary's, Norwich', *Baptist quarterly* **8**, 1936-7, 326-31. Description of the church's records.

Congregationalists

BROWNE, JOHN. *History of Congregationalism, and memorials of the churches in Norfolk and Suffolk.* Jarrold and Sons, 1877. Includes extensive lists of ministers, with notes on each church.

'Conventicles in East Anglia, 1669', *Transactions of the Congregational History Society* **2**, 1905-6, 282-5. List with some names.

THORPE, A.F. 'From the Guestwick church book, 1692-1732', *Transactions of the Congregational History Society* **16**, 1949-51, 190-202. Includes 25 biographical notes on individuals mentioned.

Huguenots/Walloons

The major work on the Dutch Church at Norwich is:

MOENS, WILLIAM JOHN CHARLES. *The Walloons and their church at Norwich: their history and registers, 1565-1832.* Publications of the Huguenot Society of London **1**, 1887-8. Includes an index to the register, rather than a transcript; also includes return of church members, 1568, extracts from lay subsidies, list of wills, return of 'strangers', 1623, transcripts of and extracts from many other documents and a detailed history.

See also:

RYE, WALTER. 'The Dutch refugees in Norwich', *N.A.M.* **3**, 1887, 185-248. Includes a list, 1568, etc.

SLAUGHTER, STEPHEN S., ed. 'The Dutch church in Norwich', *Transactions of the Congregational History Society* **12**, 1933-6, 31-48 & 81-96. Documents from the *Book of orders for strangers in Norwich*; includes some names.

SMITH, LUCY TOULMIN 'The Walloon church in Norwich in 1589', *N.A.M.* **2**, 1883, 91-148. Includes names, 16-17th c.

LART, CHARLES E. 'Some passive resisters of 1612', *Ancestor* **12**, Dec. 1904, 104-10. Huguenots at Norwich.

MOENS, W.J.C. 'Norwich Dutch Church Company of Militia in 1621', *East Anglian* N.S. **1**, 1885-6, 265-7. List.

'Dutch Congregation, Norwich: list of members, cir 1677', *East Anglian* N.S. **1**, 1885-6, 58-60.

'Huguenot records: a postscript', *Archives* **11**(52), 1974, 211-12. Summary of conference discussion, concerning records in Kent, Southampton, and Norfolk.

Methodists

PALGRAVE-MOORE, PATRICK. 'Methodist genealogical research in Norwich', *N.Anc.* 2(4), 1981, 52. Brief note on history and records.

Quakers

'First publishers of truth in Norwich', *Journal of the Friends Historical Society* 18, 1921, 22-5. Includes list of names, c.1654.

EDDINGTON, ARTHUR J. *The first fifty years of Quakerism in Norwich*. Friend Historical Society, 1932. Includes a list of Norwich Friends in 1700, and various other name lists, etc.

LLOYD-PRICHARD, MURIEL F. 'Norfolk Friends care of their poor, 1700-1850', *Journal of the Friends Historical Society* 39, 1947, 18-32 & 40, 1948, 3-19. General discussion; includes useful list of manuscript sources.

EDDINGTON, ARTHUR J. 'The quarterly meeting of Norfolk', *Journal of the Friends Historical Society* 33, 1936, 35-49; 34, 1937, 48-58 & 35, 1938, 70-78. Includes list of 18th c. clerks.

Roman Catholics

TRAPPES-LOMAX, T.B. 'Roman Catholicism in Norfolk, 1559-1780', *N.A.* 32, 1961, 27-46. Includes list of Catholic families.

M., R.W. 'Papists in East Anglia in 1585', *E.A.M.* 1911, 17-18. List.

'Popish and sectary recusants in Norfolk and Suffolk, 1596', *East Anglian* 2, 1865, 159-60 & 176-82.

C., J.L. 'Refusal of Roman Catholics to take the oath of allegiance', *East Anglian* N.S. 7, 1897-8, 285-8. List of those fined in 1745 in Cambridgeshire, Suffolk, Essex and Norfolk.

HOLT, T.G. 'Catholic chapels in Norwich before 1900: secular and Jesuit', *N.A.* 35, 1980, 153-68. Includes lists of clergy.

Jews

LIPMAN, V.D. *The Jews of medieval Norwich.* Jewish Historical Society of England, 1967. Includes many medieval deeds, etc.

DAVIS, M.D. 'East Anglians in early Hebrew deeds', *East Anglian* N.S. 4-5, 1891-4, passim. Mainly concerns Norwich.

15. ESTATE RECORDS

A. *GENERAL*

The records of estate administration constitute a mine of information for the genealogist. Much is in print, although far more lies untouched in the archives. A list of manorial rolls in the British Library (formerly the British Museum) is printed in:

STEDMAN, A.E. 'East Anglian manor court rolls: Mss. Department of the British Museum', *East Anglian* N.S. 13, 1909-10, 22-4. Covers Suffolk, Norfolk, Essex and Cambridgeshire.

A number of substantial editions of Norfolk deed abstracts are available. A general discussion of 'feet of fines', i.e. medieval deeds, with particular reference to Norfolk, is provided by:

RYE, WALTER. 'Feet of fines', *Genealogist* 6, 1882, 229-36.

Editions of feet of fines include:

DODWELL, BARBARA, ed. *Feet of fines for the County of Norfolk for the tenth year of the reign of King Richard the First, 1198-1199, and for the first four years of the reign of King John, 1199-1202.* Pipe Roll Society publications 65, N.S. 27, 1952.

DODWELL, BARBARA, ed. *Feet of fines for the County of Norfolk for the reign of King John, 1201-1215, for the County of Suffolk for the reign of King John, 1199-1214.* Pipe Roll Society publications 70, N.S. 32, 1956.

RYE, WALTER, ed. *Pedes finium relating to the County of Norfolk levied in the Kings court from the third year of Richard I to the end of the reign of John.* Norwich: A.H. Goose, 1881. Issued with *Norfolk Archaeology*. Completes the work of the same title commenced by G.H. Dashwood, in 1863, which is reproduced here in tabular form.

RYE, WALTER, ed. *A short calendar of feet of fines for Norfolk ...* 2 vols. Norwich: A.H. Goose, 1885-6. v.1. Richard I—Edward I. v.2. Edward II—Richard III.

RYE, WALTER. 'Norfolk fines', *East Anglian* 2, 1866, 183-5. Brief index, 1507-16.

RYE, WALTER. 'Rough indexes nominum to the feet of fines for Norfolk for the reign of Henry VIII, Edward VI and Mary', *N.A.M.* 2, 1883, 195-216.

Other published collections of deed abstracts and indexes include:

TINGEY, J.C. 'A calendar of deeds enrolled within the county of Norfolk', *N.A.* 13, 1898, 33-92, 125-91 & 241-92. 16-18th c.

Estate Records continued

A. GENERAL continued

RYE, WALTER. 'Norfolk deeds preserved in the Common Pleas (Com. Banco), 1504-1629', *East Anglian* **2**, 1866, 251-5. Index.

'Licences and pardons, Alienation Office', in SELBY, WALFORD D., ed. *Norfolk records* **1**. Norwich: Agas H. Goose, 1886, 93-155. Topographical index, with personal names, to records of lands etc. purchased from the crown.

'Palmer's index locorum to the patent rolls, Henry VIII to Charles II', in SELBY, WALFORD D., ed. *Norfolk records* **1**. Norwich: Agas H. Goose, 1886, 156-221. Topographical index to crown grants, especially of ex-monastic lands.

BIDEN, L.M., & WRIGHT, H.A., eds. 'Calendar of fee-farm rents: Norfolk', *East Anglian* N.S. **10**, 1903-4, 165-7, 181-3, 226-8 & 236-8; **11**, 1905-6, 10-12. Grants of monastic property, 16th c.

For the Bedford Level registry of deeds, see:

TATE, W.E. 'The five English district statutory registers of deeds', *Bulletin of the Institute of Historical Research* **20**, 1943-5, 97-105. Includes Bedford Level, which covered the Isle of Ely, large parts of Huntingdonshire, Norfolk and Suffolk, and smaller areas in Northamptonshire and Lincolnshire; also Middlesex and Yorkshire.

A number of antiquaries' and booksellers' collections of deeds have been published:

'The value of old parchment documents in genealogical and topographical research', *Genealogical quarterly* **4**, 1935-6, 48-71. Abstracts of deeds from a bookseller's collection.

STEPHEN, G.A. 'Norfolk deeds in the Greenwell collection, Public Reference Library, Newcastle on Tyne', reprinted from *N.A.* **23**(2), 1928, 265-8.

STEPHEN, GEO. A. 'Norfolk deeds in the Jackson collection, Public Reference Library, Sheffield', *N.A.* **23**, 1929, 11-15. Deed extracts, mainly medieval.

B. PRIVATE ESTATES

The larger proprietors in Norfolk had lands in various parts of the county, and sometimes in other counties as well. The estate papers of a number of families have been listed and published:

B. PRIVATE ESTATES continued

Bacon

SMITH, A. HASSELL, BAKER, GILLIAN M., & KENNY, R.W., eds. *The papers of Nathaniel Bacon of Stiffkey*. 3 vols. N.R.S. **46**, 1979, **49**, 1983 and **53**, 1988. v.1. 1556-1577. v.2. 1578-1585. v.3. 1586-1595. Includes letters, estate papers, records of local administration, etc., 1556-95.

PREST, WILFRID. 'An Australian holding of Norfolk manuscripts: the Bacon-Townshend papers at the University of Adelaide', *N.A.* **37**, 1980, 121-3. Brief note on a stray collection of family papers.

Capell

'The manuscripts of the Earl of Essex preserved at Casiobury Park, Watford', in HISTORICAL MANUSCRIPTS COMMISSION *Report on manuscripts in various collections, vol.VII*. Cd.6722. H.M.S.O., 1914, 297-350. Papers relating to the estates of the Capell family in Hertfordshire, Essex and Norfolk, etc., medieval-17th c.

De Grey

CRABBE, G. 'Report of the muniments at Merton Hall, Norfolk', *N.A.M.* **2**, 1883, 553-629, **3**, 1887, 1-113. Relating to the family of De Grey, medieval-19th c., and the manors of Merton, Bunwell, Ellingham Magna, Thompson, Tottington, Stanford, Sturston, Ickburgh, Watton and Griston in Norfolk, and of Cornard, Copdock and Washbrook in Suffolk.

Hobart

HISTORICAL MANUSCRIPTS COMMISSION *Report on the manuscripts of the Marquis of Lothian preserved at Blickling Hall, Norfolk*. Cd.2319. H.M.S.O., 1905. Lists numerous deeds, court rolls, etc., relating to property in various parishes, also includes transcript of 1663 subsidy, and letters, etc., of the Hobart family, 17th c.

Howard

RIGG, J.M. 'Ancient deeds belonging to the Duke of Norfolk, K.G., and relating chiefly to manors in the counties of Norfolk and Suffolk', in HISTORICAL MANUSCRIPTS COMMISSION *Report on manuscripts in various collections*. vol.VII. Cd.6722. H.M.S.O., 1914, 153-246.

STEER, FRANCIS W., ed. *Arundel Castle archives*. 4 vols. Chichester: West Sussex County Council, 1968-80. Includes some Norfolk material relating to the Howard family.

B. *PRIVATE ESTATES continued*

Leicester

JESSOPP, AUGUSTUS. 'Charters, early conveyances, court rolls, &c., of the Right Hon. the Earl of Leicester, preserved at Holkham Hall, Norfolk', in HISTORICAL MANUSCRIPTS COMMISSION *Ninth report ... Part 1: report and appendix.* C.3773. H.M.S.O., 1883, 313-25. Mainly relating to medieval Norfolk.

Walpole

CHINNERY, GILBERT ALLEN, ed. *A handlist of the Cholmondeley (Houghton) mss: Sir Robert Walpole's archive.* Cambridge: University Library, 1953. Includes estate papers, 14-18th c.

YAXLEY, DAVID, ed. *Survey of the Houghton Hall estate by Joseph Hill, 1800.* N.R.S. **50**, 1984. Survey for the Earl of Cholmondeley of the Walpole family estate he inherited; gives names of tenants.

C. *ECCLESIASTICAL ESTATES*

Ecclesiastical estates were of great importance, especially prior to the Reformation; further, their records have a much greater chance of survival than the records of private families, since they were 'perpetual' institutions. Their deeds were frequently collected together into chartularies, many of which have been published. These, together with other ecclesiastical estate records, are listed here.

Blackbergh Nunnery

COOKE, A.H. 'Five compotus rolls of Blackbergh Nunnery', *N.A.* **22**, 1926, 83-5. Brief description.

Blackborough Priory

COLLINS, A.J. 'The Blackborough chartulary at the library of Sir Henry Spelman', *British Museum quarterly* **11**, 1936-7, 63-5. Brief description of Blackborough Priory's chartulary.

Bromholm Priory

REDSTONE, LILIAN J., ed. *Cellarer's roll, Bromholm Priory, 1415-1416.* N.R.S. **17**, 1944, 45-91. Gives names of many tenants, tradesmen, etc.

Carrow Abbey

RYE, WALTER. *Carrow Abbey, otherwise Carrow Priory: its foundation, buildings, officers & inmates. With appendices: charters, proceedings, extracts from wills, landed possessions, founders, architectural description of the remains of the buildings, and some account of the family of the present owners.* Norwich: A.H. Goose, 1889. Includes an account of the Colman family.

RYE, WALTER, & TILLETT, EDWARD A. 'Carrow Abbey', *N.A.* **2**, 1883, 465-508. Includes list of prioresses, estates, deed abstracts, etc., with pedigree of Rye, medieval.

Crabhouse Nunnery

BATESON, MARY. 'The register of Crabhouse Nunnery', *N.A.M.* **11**, 1892, 1-71.

Creake Abbey

BEDINGFELD, A.L., ed. *A cartulary of Creake Abbey.* N.R.S. **35**, 1966.

Hempton Priory

L'ESTRANGE, JOHN. 'The account of the bursar of Hempton Priory for the year 1500-1', *N.A.M.* **1**, 1877, 107-40. Gives many names.

Holme Abbey

WEST, J.R., ed. *St.Benet of Holme, 1020-1210: the eleventh and twelfth century sections of Cott. ms. Galba E.ii, the register of the Abbey of St.Benet of Holme.* 2 vols. N.R.S. **2-3**, 1932. Chartulary; the final volume consists wholly of introductory material.

HOWLETT, R. 'Account rolls of certain of the obedientaries of the Abbey of St.Benedict at Holme', *N.A.M.* **2**, 1883, 530-49. 1440-41; includes some names of tenants, etc.

Lewes Priory, Sussex

BULLOCK, J.H., ed. *The Norfolk portion of the chartulary of the priory of St.Pancras of Lewes.* N.R.S. **12**, 1939.

Norwich. Cathedral Priory

DODWELL, BARBARA, ed. *The charters of Norwich Cathedral Priory.* 2 vols. Pipe Roll Society publications **78** & **84**, N.S. **40** & **46**, 1974-8. Chartulary.

SAUNDERS, H.W., ed. *The first register of Norwich Cathedral Priory.* N.R.S. **11**, 1939. Chartulary; ends 1300.

C. *ECCLESIASTICAL ESTATES continued*
Norwich. Cathedral Priory *continued*

SAUNDERS, H.W. *An introduction to the obedientiary & manor rolls of Norwich Cathedral Priory.* Norwich: Jarrold & Sons, 1930. General discussion of manorial rolls relating to property throughout the county; includes lists of priors and obedientiaries.

SAUNDERS, H.W. 'A problem in 'wandered' mss.', *Discovery* **11**, 1930, 79-81. Discussion of a survey of Norwich Cathedral manors, late 13th c.

METTERS, G.A., ed. *The Parliamentary survey of Dean and Chapter properties in and around Norwich in 1649.* N.R.S. **51**, 1985. Includes notes on the Cathedral Close by Arthur Whittingham.

Norwich. St.Leonard's Priory

BENSLY, W.T. 'St.Leonard's Priory, Norwich', *N.A.* **12**, 1895, 190-227.

Oxford. New College

RICKARD, R.L., ed. *The progress notes of Warden Woodward, 1659-1675, and other 17th century documents, relating to the Norfolk property of New College, Oxford.* N.R.S. **22**, 1951, 85-115.

Ramsey Abbey, Huntingdonshire

HART, WILLIAM HENRY, & LYONS, PONSONBY A., eds. *Cartularium monasterii de Rameseia.* 3 vols. Rolls series **79**, H.M.S.O., 1884-93. Includes deeds, etc., relating to much Norfolk property.

AULT, WARREN ORTMAN, ed. *Court rolls of the Abbey of Ramsey and the Honour of Clare.* New Haven: Yale University Press; London: Oxford University Press, 1928. 13th c. rolls of the Honours of Broughton, Huntingdonshire and Clare, Suffolk, the Banlieu of Ramsey Abbey, Huntingdonshire, and the Norfolk Hundred of Clackclose and Leet of Walsoken.

BIRCH, W. DE G. 'Historical notes on the manuscripts belonging to Ramsey Abbey', *Journal of the British Archaeological Association* N.S. **5**, 1899, 229-42. Includes lists of rolls, deeds, etc. for properties in Huntingdonshire and many other counties, including Norfolk.

Rushford

BENNET, E.K. 'The College of S.John Evangelist of Rushford, Co.Norfolk', *N.A.* **10**, 1888, 277-382. Reprinted Norwich: A.H. Goose & Co., 1887. Includes calendar of deeds, and medieval pedigrees of Monchensy, Lerling and Gonvile.

C. *ECCLESIASTICAL ESTATES continued*
Shouldham Priory

'Charters to Shouldham Priory', *Genealogist* N.S. **36**, 1920, 74-7. Medieval.

Thetford Priory

HARVEY, JOHN H. 'Building works by an East Anglian priory', *N.A.* **35**, 1973, 505-10. Includes 15-16th c. extracts from accounts of Thetford Priory, giving names.

D. *RECORDS OF INDIVIDUAL MANORS*

Banham
See Bradcar

Bradcar

HUDSON, WILLIAM. 'Three manorial extents of the thirteenth century', *N.A.* **14**, 1901, 1-56. For Bradcar and Banham in Norfolk, and Wykes, Suffolk.

Cossey

STEVENSON, JOSEPH. 'The manuscripts of Lord Stafford, of Cossey Hall, Norfolk', in HISTORICAL MANUSCRIPTS COMMISSION *The manuscripts of the Earl of Westmorland, Captain Stewart, Lord Stafford, Lord Muncaster, and others.* 10th report, appendix, pt.4. H.M.S.O., 1885, 152-68. Estate papers relating to the manor of Cossey, 13-18th c.

Denton
See Redenhall and Topcroft

East Dereham

HOLLIS, D.W. 'A mid-seventeenth century view of East Dereham manor', *N.A.* **36**, 1977, 342-54. Parliamentary survey, 1649, including a rental.

Forncett

DAVENPORT, FRANCES GARDINER. *The economic development of a Norfolk manor (Forncett), 1086-1565.* Cambridge: C.U.P., 1906. Reprinted Frank Cass & Co., 1967. Includes list of mss. relating to the manor, abstract of 1565 survey, lay subsidy, 1332, table of leases, 1401-1500, etc., etc.

Gaywood

BRADFER-LAWRENCE, H.L. 'Gaywood Dragge, 1486-7', *N.A.* **24**, 1932, 146-83. Terrier naming many tenants.

Estate Records continued

C. *INDIVIDUAL MANORS continued*

Gimingham

HOARE, CHRISTOBEL M. *The history of an East Anglian soke: studies in original documents.* Bedford: Beds. Times, 1918. Deals with Gimingham; includes many extracts from manorial court rolls, a chapter on family names which includes pedigrees, and a list of rectors.

HOARE, CHRISTOBEL M. 'The last of the bondmen in a Norfolk manor', *N.A.* **19**, 1917, 9-32. Includes list of 23 bondmen manumitted in Gimingham during Elizabeth I's reign.

Great Cressington

CHANDLER, HENRY W., ed. *Five court rolls of Great Cressington in the county of Norfolk.* Eyre and Spottiswoode, 1885. 1328-1584; includes rental, 1414.

Great Frensham

See Mills on the Moor

Great Yarmouth

See Kings Lynn

Hempstead

See Horstead

Hevingham

CAMPBELL, BRUCE M.S. 'The complexity of manorial structure in medieval Norfolk: a cast study', *N.A.* **38**, 1986, 225-61. Based on a township survey of Hevingham, 1279.

Horsford

BARRETT-LEONARD, SIR THOMAS. 'Two hundred years of estate management at Horsford during the 17th and 18th centuries', *N.A.* **20**, 1921, 57-139. Includes rent roll, 1613.

Horstead

CORBETT, W.J. 'Elizabethan village surveys', *Transactions of the Royal Historical Society* N.S. **11**, 1897, 67-87. Discussion of surveys at Kings College, Cambridge; includes lists of tenants, 1374, at Horstead, Hempstead and Lessingham.

Ingham

FARROW, CHARLES. 'Two Norfolk tithe accounts', *N.Anc.* **1**(10), 1980, 134-5. Lists proprietors and occupiers at Ingham, 1831, and Southery, 1838.

Kings Lynn

RUTLEDGE, ELIZABETH, & RUTLEDGE, PAUL. 'Kings Lynn and Great Yarmouth: two thirteenth-century surveys', *N.A.* **35**, 1980, 92-114. Probably prepared for royal purposes.

Lessingham

See Horstead

Mattishall

CRISP, F.A. *Genealogical abstracts of deeds relating to families connected with the parishes of Mattishall and Reepham in the county of Norfolk.* F.A. Crisp, 1885.

PRICHARD, M.F. LLOYD. 'The vicar of Mattishall and his tithes, 1781-1803', *Agricultural history* **27**, 1953, 141-7. Includes a list of tenants of the Rectory in Mattishall and Bergh, 1781.

Mills on the Moor

FARRAR, J. MICHAEL. 'Manor of Mills on the Moor, together with Great Frensham (Norfolk)', *Genealogical quarterly* **23**(2), 1956, 89-91. 1670 leet roll.

RUNDLE, C.A. 'A closer look at manorial records', *Genealogical quarterly* **31**(2), 1964, 57-9. Rental of Mills on the Moor and Great Frensham, 1780.

North Runcton

'Manor court papers of North Runcton and Setchey', *East Anglian* N.S. **3**, 1889-90, 41-5. Mid-17th c.

Norwich

RYE, WALTER, ed. *A short calendar of the deeds relating to Norwich enrolled in the court rolls of that city, 1285-1306.* Norwich: Norfolk & Norwich Archaeological Society, 1903.

RYE, WALTER, ed. *A calendar of Norwich deeds enrolled in the court rolls of that city, 1307-1341.* Norwich: Norfolk & Norwich Archaeological Society, 1915.

PRIESTLEY, URSULA, ed. *Men of property: an analysis of the Norwich enrolled deeds, 1285-1311.* Norwich: Centre of East Anglian Studies, 1984. Useful discussion of the deeds as a source.

Redenhall

'Admission to manors in Redenhall & Denton, Co.Norfolk', *Fragmenta genealogica* **4**, 1899, 35-6.

Reepham

See Mattishall

Southery

See Ingham

C. *INDIVIDUAL MANORS continued*
Stiffkey
BRADFER-LAWRENCE, H.L. 'Stiffkey alias Stewkey', *N.A.* **23**, 1929, 308-40. Includes terrier, c.1300, naming tenants, with inventory of Sir Roger Townshend, 1636.

Stockton
MARSHALL, GEORGE W. 'Extracts from manor court rolls: Stockton with the Soke', *East Anglian* **4**, 1871, 3-4, 13-15 & 25-8. 17th c.

Topcroft
CANDLER, CHARLES. 'List of tenants in the manor of Topcroft with Denton: survey 32 Elizabeth', *East Anglian* N.S. **8**, 1899-1900, 10.

CANDLER, CHARLES. 'Notes from an extent of the manor of Topcroft with Denton, Co.Norfolk, dated April 1491', *East Anglian* N.S. **7**, 1897-8, 193-7. Includes list of tenants.

Wells next the Sea
BLOOMFIELD, G. 'Names in Wells-next-the-Sea enclosure award dated 1st Oct., 1813', *S.Rt.* **5**(4), 1979, 66-7.

E. *MANORIAL AND OTHER DESCENTS*
The descents of many manors have been traced— several of the works listed in section 1 above provide much information on manorial lords. Many brief descents are also given in:

RYE, WALTER. *Castles and manor houses from the Conquest to the present time.* Rye's *Norfolk handlists* 1st series, **3**. Norwich: Roberts & Co., 1916.

WILLINS, EDWARD PRESTON. *Some of the old halls and manor-houses in the county of Norfolk.* Jarrold & Sons, 1890.

A number of works include information relating to the descent of particular properties:

Breccles Hall
JESSOPP, AUGUSTUS. 'Notes on the history of Breccles Hall, Norfolk', *N.A.* **8**, 1879, 303-15. Descent, 16-19th c., concerns Woodhouse family, 16th c., includes pedigree of Webbe, 17-18th c., Taylor, 18-19th c., etc.

Easthall
DASHWOOD, GEORGE HENRY. 'Particulars of Easthall manor house in Denver with notices of its several proprietors', *N.A.* **3**, 1852, 125-33. Manorial descent; includes folded pedigree of Manby of Middleton, Yorkshire, Elsham, Lincolnshire, and Hilgay, Norfolk, medieval-19th c.

E. *MANORIAL AND OTHER DESCENTS*
continued
Eynsford
SAYER, MICHAEL. 'Eynsford houses', *N.A.* **35**, 1973, 213-32. See also 433. Gives descents of many properties.

Great Yarmouth
PALMER, CHARLES JOHN. *The perlustration of Great Yarmouth, with Gorleston and Southtown.* 3 vols. Great Yarmouth: George Nall, 1872-5. Includes many descents of property, notes on occupants, etc.

Hempstead
ROGERSON, ANDREW, & ADAMS, NICK. 'A moated site at Hempstead, near Holt', *East Anglian archaeology: report* **8**, 1978, 55-72. Includes notes on medieval descent.

Horsford
BARRETT-LEONARD, THOMAS. 'Some account of the manor or castle of Horsford', *N.A.* **15**, 1904, 267-92. Includes pedigree showing descent of the manor through many families.

Little Ellingham
TINGEY, J.C. 'The manorial history of Little Ellingham', *N.A.* **21**, 1923, 1-32. Descent of the manor.

Mannington Hall
TOMES, CHARLES S. *Mannington Hall and its owners.* Norwich: Goose & Son, 1916. Descent through Tyrel, Lumnor, Potts and Walpole, medieval-19th c.

Norwich
RYE, WALTER. *Norwich houses before 1600.* Rye's *Norfolk handlists* 1st series, **4**. Norwich: Roberts & Co., 1916. Traces many descents.

CRESCENT HISTORY GROUP *The Crescent, Norwich: listing of occupiers, 1825-1978.* Norwich: Crescent History Group, 1978. Identifies all residents in each house.

Shelfanger
HARRISON, W.R. 'Notes on the early lords of manors in the parish of Shelfanger', *N.A.* **20**, 1921, 31-56. Medieval descents.

Pockthorpe
BULWER, JAMES. 'Hassett's House, Pockthorpe, Norwich', *N.A.* **7**, 1872, 79-92. Traces descent, includes will of William Blennerhassett, 1598.

E. *MANORIAL AND OTHER DESCENTS*
continued
Rockland Tofts
MUSKETT, J.J. 'Pedigree illustrating the descent of Ladies Manor, Rockland Tofts: Moriel, Sibbs, Muskett, Blomefield', *East Anglian* N.S. **4**, 1891-92, 9-11. See also 35-6. 16-17th c.

16. RECORDS OF NATIONAL AND COUNTY ADMINISTRATION

Official lists of names, such as tax lists and muster rolls, have already been discussed. There are, however, many other records of central and county government which provide useful information. A number of publications list the holders of important offices:

LE STRANGE, HAMON. *Norfolk official lists from the earliest period to the present day compiled from original sources*. Norwich: Agas H. Goose, 1890. Lists M.P's, sheriffs, ecclesiastical dignitaries, mayors, recorders, etc. for the county and its boroughs.

EWING, W.C. *Norfolk lists from the Reformation to the present time, comprising lists of Lord Lieutenants, baronets, high sheriffs and members of parliament* ... Norwich: Matchett, Stevenson and Matchett, 1837.

[DASHWOOD, GEORGE HENRY.] *Vicecomites Norfolciae, or, Sheriffs of Norfolk from the first year of Henry the Second, to the fourth of Queen Victoria, inclusive* ... Stow Bardolph, 1843. Continued in *East Anglian* N.S. **1**, 1885-6, 201-3.

ATHILL, CHARLES. 'Vicecomites Norfolcioe, or, Sheriffs of Norfolk', *East Anglian* N.S. **1**, 1885-6, 201-3. List, 1837-85, with arms.

LANDON, L. 'The sheriffs of Norfolk', *N.A.* **23**, 1929, 147-65. List, with biographical notes, 11-12th c. Includes pedigree showing descent of Carbrook and Saxlingham manors to the Munchensy family, 11-14th c.

ROUND, J.H. 'The early sheriffs of Norfolk', *English Historical Review* **35**, 1920, 481-96. General discussion, with genealogical notes.

MCKISACK, MAY. 'The Parliamentary representation of Kings Lynn', *English Historical Review* **42**, 1927, 582-9. Includes list of M.P's not given in the *Official list of Members of Parliament*.

Many transcripts, calendars, indexes, etc. of useful records have been published, and are listed here in rough chronological order:

POTTER, GEORGE RICHARD. *Translation of so much of the pipe roll of 31 Henry I as relates to Norfolk and Suffolk*. Rye's Norfolk handlists, 2nd series, **2**. Norwich: H.W. Hunt, 1925.

RYE, WALTER. 'Crime and accident in Norfolk in the time of Henry III and Edward I', *N.A.M.* **2**, 1883, 159-93. Extracts from Plea Rolls relating to the Hundred of North Erpingham. Many names.

National and County Admin. continued

BLAKE, WILLIAM J. 'Norfolk manorial lords in 1316', *N.A.* **30**, 1952, 235-86. Analysis of the Nomina Villarum, with a translation.

'Index locorum to the De Banco rolls, Edward II (A.D. 1307 to A.D. 1327)', in SELBY, WALFORD D., ed. *Norfolk records* **1**. Norwich: Agas H. Goose, 1886, 222-65. Topographical index to pleadings in the Court of Common Pleas.

RYE, WALTER. 'Crime in Norfolk, temp. Edward III', *East Anglian* **3**, 1869, 148-53. From a roll of crown pleas and gaol delivery, 1332. Many names.

REDSTONE, LILIAN J., ed. 'Norfolk sessions of the peace: roll of mainpernors and pledges, 1394-1397', N.R.S. **8**, 1936, 1-14.

'Norfolk gentry in 1433 and 1523', *N.A.M.* **2**, 1883, 393-8. List of gentry made in a return to the Crown of 1433 and in the 1523 subsidy.

'List of Exchequer bills and answers, Elizabeth (A.D. 1558-1603)', in SELBY, WALFORD D., ed. *Norfolk records* **1**. Norwich: Agas H. Goose, 1886, 266-93.

SAUNDERS, H.W., ed. *The official papers of Sir Nathaniel Bacon of Stiffkey, Norfolk, as Justice of the Peace, 1580-1620.* Camden 3rd series **26**, Royal Historical Society, 1915.

BROOKS, F.W. 'Supplementary Stiffkey papers', in *Camden miscellany* **16**, Camden 3rd series **52**, Royal Historical Society, 1936. 1578-1620.

ROSENHEIM, JAMES M., ed. *The notebook of Robert Doughty, 1662-1665.* N.R.S. **54**, 1989. Notebook of a J.P., recording cases that came before him.

JAMES, D.E. HOWELL. *Norfolk quarter sessions order book, 1650-1657.* N.R.S. **26**, 1955.

MORANT, ALFRED W. 'Notes on a letter and declaration of the gentry of Norfolk and Norwich to General Monk', *N.A.* **7**, 1872, 309-20. Biographical note on signatories, 1660.

An address from the gentry of Norfolk and Norwich to General Monck in 1660: facsimile of a manuscript in the Norwich Public Library. Norwich: Jarrold & Sons, 1913. Includes list of signatories, with biographical notes by Walter Rye.

ROSENHEIM, JAMES M., ed. *The notebook of Robert Doughty, 1662-1665.* N.R.S. **54**, 1989. Notebook of a Justice of the Peace.

JONES, HONOR. 'Norfolk game duty certificates, 1800', *N.Anc.* **2**(12), 1983, 163-7. Extensive list of certificates issued; also for Norwich, 1802.

JONES, HONOR. 'Norfolk game duty: registered gamekeepers, 1801', *N.Anc.* **4**(7), 1987, 109-12 & **4**(9), 1987, 153-5. Listed, with names of manorial lords.

17. RECORDS OF BOROUGH AND PAROCHIAL ADMINISTRATION

Parochial administration in the pre-industrial age resulted in the creation of a wide range of documents—churchwardens' accounts, rate lists, overseers' accounts, settlement examinations, etc. It is unlikely that there were many whose names went totally unrecorded in these documents. For Norfolk, many extracts, calendars, transcripts, etc. have been published, and are listed here by parish. For parish registers, see section 8.

Alburgh
COOPER, E.R. 'Alburgh: churchwardens' and overseers' accounts, 1622-92', *E.A.M.* **1933**, 47. Brief note.

Barton Turf
'Barton Turf rate book', *N.N.N.Q.* 2nd series, 1899-1904, 345-6. See also 347-8 & 354. Brief 18th c. extracts.

Blakeney
COZENS-HARDY, B., ed. 'The maritime trade of the port of Blakeney, which included Cley and Wiveton, 1587 to 1590', N.R.S. **8**, 1936, 17-37. Port book, giving names of many ships' masters and merchants.

Cley
See Blakeney

Diss
JEAFFRESON, JOHN CORDY. 'The manuscripts of the Reverend C.R. Manning, M.A., rector of Diss, Norfolk', in HISTORICAL MANUSCRIPTS COMMISSION *Tenth report, appendix, part IV*. H.M.S.O., 1885, 458-63. Records from the parish chest.

Great Yarmouth
The Great Yarmouth borough archives are fully listed in:
RUTLEDGE, PAUL. *Guide to the Great Yarmouth borough records*. Norfolk & Norwich Record Office, 1972.

See also:
HARROD, HENRY. *Repertory of deeds and documents relating to the Borough of Great Yarmouth in the county of Norfolk*. Great Yarmouth: Town Council, 1855.
JEAFFRESON, JOHN CORDY. 'The manuscripts of the Corporation of Great Yarmouth, Co. Norfolk', in HISTORICAL MANUSCRIPTS COMMISSION *Ninth report ... Part.1: report and appendix*. C.3773. H.M.S.O., 1883, 299-324.

Great Yarmouth *continued*
HARROD, HENRY. 'Notes on the records of the Corporation of Great Yarmouth', *N.A.* **4**, 1855, 239-66.
Bailiffs
RUTLEDGE, PAUL. 'The earliest Yarmouth bailiffs', *N.A.* **40**, 1989, 181-5. List, 13th c.
Charities
Report upon the charities of the Borough of Great Yarmouth. Great Yarmouth: George Nall, 1876. Includes many extracts from deeds, wills, surveys, etc.
Freemen
[DE CHAIR, BEAUCHAMP, ed.] *A calendar of the freemen of Great Yarmouth, 1429-1800*. Norwich: Norfolk & Norwich Archaeological Society, 1910. Chronological list of freemen.
Minute Book
RUTLEDGE, P., ed. 'Great Yarmouth assembly minutes, 1538-1545', N.R.S. **39**, 1970, 1-80.

Harleston
See Redenhall

Holt
HALES, JANE. 'Settlement stories', *N.A.* **35**, 1973, 126-30. Discussion of 81 settlement examinations, 1759-1836, from Holt.

Kings Lynn
The archives of Kings Lynn are listed in two works:
HISTORICAL MANUSCRIPTS COMMISSION *The manuscripts of the corporation of Southampton and Kings Lynn*. 11th report, appendix, pt.3. Cd.5060-ii. H.M.S.O., 1887.
HARROD, H. *Report on the deeds & records of the borough of Kings Lynn*. Kings Lynn: Thew & Son, 1874.

Many valuable documents are printed in:
OWEN, DOROTHY M. *The making of King's Lynn: a documentary survey*. Records of social and economic history, N.S. **9**. O.U.P. for the British Academy, 1984. Includes many original documents, e.g. Bede roll of the gild of Holy Trinity, 13-15th c. (lists names), obit roll of the hospital of St.Mary Magdalen, accounts, court rolls, deeds, etc., etc.
INGLEBY, HOLCOMBE, ed. *The red register of King's Lynn,* transcribed by R.F. Isaacson. 2 vols. Kings Lynn: Thew & Son, 1919-22. A typescript index is available at the British Library. Includes many deeds, wills, etc., medieval.

For freemen, see:

Borough and Parochial Admin. *continued*

Kings Lynn *continued*

A calendar of the freemen of Lynn, 1292-1836.
Norwich: Norfolk & Norwich Archaeological
Society, 1913. Chronological list.

A variety of other works provide transcripts of,
and extracts from, a wide variety of administrative
documents:

BELOE, EDWARD MILLIGAN, ed. *Extracts from the
chapel wardens' accounts of St.Nicholas'
Chapel, Kings Lynn, from the year 1616 to the
date of the restoration of ... Charles the Second.*
Kings Lynn: E.M. Beloe, 1926.

BELOE, EDWARD MILLIGAN, ed. *The Guildhall Court
of Kings Lynn.* Kings Lynn: the author, 1923.
Includes extracts from records, 17th c.

BULWER, JAMES. 'Notice of a manuscript volume
among the records of the Corporation of Lynn',
N.A. **6**, 1864, 217-49. Includes lists of
burgesses, 15th c.

DASHWOOD, G.H., ed. 'Extracts from the
Chamberlain's book of accounts, 14 Hen IV, in
the possession of the Corporation of Lynn
Regis', *N.A.* **2**, 1849, 183-92.

FYSH, A.V.G.A. 'King's Lynn poor law records',
N.Anc. **4**(1), 1985, 8. List of men impressed,
1755.

GURNEY, HUDSON. 'Extracts from a manuscript
containing portions of the proceedings of the
Corporation of Lynn Regis, in Norfolk, from
1430 to 1731, taken from the hall books',
Archaeologia **24**, 1932, 317-28. Includes many
names of mayors, merchants, members of
parliament, etc., mainly 15-16th c.

EDWARDS, STANLEY, ed. 'Strangers at Lynn in
1572', *N.A.M.* **1**, 1877, 195-8. Contemporary
list; the names are mainly English, but a list of
Scots is appended.

HOWLETT, RICHARD. 'The early bede roll of the
merchants' guild at Lynn, containing the name
of John Chaucer', *N.A.M.* 2nd series **3**, 1908,
29-79. Lists 850 medieval names.

OWEN, DOROTHY M., ed. 'William Asshebourne's
book: Kings Lynn corporation archives 10/2',
N.R.S. **48**, 1981, 54-103 & 111-17.
Memorandum book of the common clerk of
Kings Lynn.

Martham

YOUNG, MICHAEL. 'The parish loaf', *Family tree
magazine* 3(2), 1986, 22. See also 3(4), 1987, 7.
The poor law in Martham, Norfolk, based on
overseers' records.

Martham *continued*

YOUNG, MICHAEL. 'A momentous year: a parochial
view of 1688', *Family tree magazine* 5(5),
1989, 34. Notes on Martham, Norfolk, parochial
records.

North Barsham

EVANS, NESTA. 'Tithe books as a source for the
local historian', *Local historian* **14**, 1980, 24-7.
Includes note on the tithe book of North
Barsham, 17th c.

North Elmham

LEGGE, AUGUSTUS GEORGE, ed. *Ancient
churchwardens' accounts in the parish of North
Elmham, from A.D. 1539 to A.D. 1577.*
Norwich: A.H. Goose, 1891.

LEGGE, A.G., ed. 'Churchwardens' accounts, North
Elmham, A.D. 1586-1714', *East Anglian* N.S.
6, 7 & 9, 1895-1902, passim.

Northwold

MILLICAN, PERCY. 'Northwold churchwardens'
accounts, 1626-1795', *N.A.* **28**, 1945, 285-95.
Description, including brief biographical notes
on persons named.

Norwich

The archives of Norwich are calendared in a
number of works:

RYE, WALTER. *A calendar of the documents
relating to the Corporation of Norwich,
preserved in the Free Library there.* Norwich:
Gibbs & Waller, 1908.

RILEY, HENRY THOMAS. 'The Corporation of the
City of Norwich', in HISTORICAL MANUSCRIPTS
COMMISSION *First report ...* C.55. H.M.S.O.,
1874, 102-4. Brief list of archives.

HUDSON, WILLIAM, & TINGEY, JOHN COTTINGHAM,
eds. *The records of the City of Norwich.* 2 vols.
Norwich: Jarrold & Sons, 1906-10. Detailed
abstracts of medieval deeds, muster roll for
1457, wills, poor law records, etc.

HUDSON, WILLIAM, & TINGEY, JOHN COTTINGHAM.
*Revised catalogue of the records of the City of
Norwich, as arranged in the muniment room in
the Castle Museum.* Norwich: Edward Burgess
and Sons, 1898.

Freemen

L'ESTRANGE, JOHN. *Calendar of the freemen of
Norwich from 1307 to 1603 (Edward II to
Elizabeth inclusive).* ed. Walter Rye. E. Stock,
1888.

MILLICAN, PERCY. *The register of the freemen of
Norwich, 1548-1713: a transcript.* Norwich:
Jarrold & Sons, 1934.

Norwich *continued*

MILLICAN, PERCY, ed. *The freemen of Norwich, 1714-1752: a transcript of the third register.* N.R.S. **23**, 1952.

'List of freemen of Norwich', *East Anglian* **4**, 1871, passim.

City Officers

A number of works list city officers:

HAWES, TIMOTHY, ed. *An index to Norwich city officers, 1453-1835.* Norfolk genealogy **21**, 1989. Also issued as N.R.S. **52**, 1986.

COZENS-HARDY, BASIL, & KENT, ERNEST A. *The mayors of Norwich, 1403 to 1835: being biographical notes on the mayors of the old corporation.* Norwich: Jarrold & Sons, 1938.

PALGRAVE-MOORE, PATRICK. *The mayors and lord mayors of Norwich, 1836-1974.* Norwich: Elvery Dowers, 1978. Includes biographies.

GRACE, MARY. 'The Chamberlains of Norwich, 1293-1835', *N.A.* **25**, 1935, 181-201. List of chamberlains.

Miscellaneous

A number of important miscellaneous documents relating to Norwich have been published, and are listed here in rough chronological order.

HUDSON, WILLIAM, ed. *Leet jurisdiction in the city of Norwich during the XIIIth and XIVth centuries, with a short notice of its later history and decline, from rolls in the possession of the Corporation.* Selden Society **5**, 1892.

HARROD, HENRY. 'Extracts from the Coroners' rolls and other documents in the record-room of the Corporation of Norwich', *N.A.* **2**, 1847, 253-79. 13th c.

GRACE, MARY, ed. *Records of the Gild of St.George in Norwich, 1389-1547.* N.R.S. **9**, 1937.

HOWLETT, RICHARD. 'A fabric roll of the Norwich Guildhall, A.D. 1410-1411', *N.A.* **15**, 1904, 164-89. Gives many names.

ESSER, RAINGARD. *Norwich strangers book, 1583-1600.* N.N.G.S., 1990.

GALLOWAY, DAVID. *Norwich, 1540-1642.* Records of early English drama. Toronto: University of Toronto Press, 1984. Contains innumerable extracts from the city archives, with detailed notes on each source. Of much wider interest than the series title suggests, although the extracts only concern the theatre.

RYE, WALTER, ed. *Depositions taken before the mayor & aldermen of Norwich, 1549-1567; Extracts from the court books of the city of Norwich, 1666-1688.* Norwich: Norfolk & Norwich Archaeological Society, 1905.

Norwich *continued*

POUND, JOHN F., ed. *The Norwich census of the poor, 1570.* N.R.S. **40**, 1971. Gives useful information on individual paupers. Important.

RICHWOOD, D.L., ed. 'The Norwich accounts for the customs on strangers goods and merchandise, 1582-1610', N.R.S. **39**, 1970, 87-111. Gives many names of 'strangers', i.e. mainly resident Dutch.

SACHSE, WILLIAM L., ed. *Minutes of the Norwich court of mayoralty, 1630-[1635].* N.R.S. **15**, 1942, & **36**, 1972.

RYE, WALTER, ed. *The Norwich rate book from Easter 1633 to Easter 1634.* Jarrold, 1903.

St.Benedict

DOMBRAIN, JAMES. 'Archaeological notes respecting the parish of St.Benedict, in the city of Norwich', *East Anglian* **4**, 1871, 49-53. List of books in the parish chest, with extracts, 17-18th c.

St.Giles

EADE, SIR PETER. *Some account of the parish of St.Giles, Norwich, with maps, parish lists, and numerous illustrations.* Norwich: Jarrold & Sons, 1886. Includes many lists, e.g. poll books, rates, etc., also monumental inscriptions, biographies, etc.

St.Peter of Mancroft

RYE, WALTER. 'St.Peter Mancroft, Norwich: its parish history in the sixteenth and seventeenth centuries', *N.A.M.* **2**, 1883, 321-63. Mainly extracts from the churchwardens' accounts.

St.Stephen

R., A.E. 'Account books of St.Stephens church and parish, Norwich', *East Anglian* N.S. **8**, 1899-1900, 34-8, 70-71, 109-11, 132-6, 172-5, 213-6, 254-6, 284-6, 312-4 & 344-7; **9**, 1901-2, 59-62, 96-9, 158-61, 189-92, 218-22, 254-8, 286-9, 316-21, 350-53 & 383-6; **10**, 1903-4, 11-14, 26-8 & 36-8. 16-18th c.

Redenhall

RAYSON, GEORGE. 'Extracts from churchwardens' books, no.17: Redenhall with Harleston, Norfolk', *East Anglian* **4**, 1871, 54-8. 16-17th c.

Salhouse

FARROW, C.W. 'A calendar of Salhouse poor law documents', *N.Anc.* **4**(3), 1986, 38-42.

Smallburgh

GOTTS, IAN. 'Workhouse records at P.R.O., Kew', *N.Anc.* **5**(4), 1989, 82-4. Discussion of the records of Smallburgh Workhouse; includes names.

Borough and Parochial Admin. *continued*

Starston

H[OPPER], E.C. *Some account of the parish of Starston, Norfolk, compiled chiefly from the ancient registers*. Norwich: Agas H. Goose & Co., 1888. Actually includes extracts from a variety of parochial records, together with monumental inscriptions, a list of churchwardens, etc.

Stockton

CARTHEW, GEORGE ALFRed. 'Extracts from a town book of the parish of Stockton, in Norfolk, containing the churchwardens' (and incidentally, other) accounts from 1625 to 1712 inclusive', *N.A.* **1**, 1847, 167-92.

Swaffham

WILLIAMS, J.F. 'The black book of Swaffham', *N.A.* **33**, 1965, 243-53. Detailed description of a 15th c. book of parish records, includes some names.

Thetford

MACRAY, W.D. 'The manuscripts of the Corporation of Thetford, Norfolk', in HISTORICAL MANUSCRIPTS COMMISSION *Report on manuscripts in various collections, vol.VII*. Cd. 6722. H.M.S.O., 1914, 119-52.

Tilney All Saints

JUKES, H.A. LLOYD. 'The Tilney papers: a noteworthy parochial collection of historical manuscripts and printed books', *N.A.* **36**, 1977, 233-40. Discusses the parochial records of Tilney All Saints.

STALLARD, A.D. *The transcript of the churchwardens' accounts of the parish of Tilney All Saints, Norfolk, 1443 to 1589*. Mitchell Hughes & Clarke, 1922.

Toft Monks

ASHBY, W.J. 'Extracts from churchwardens' accounts, Toft Monks, Norfolk', *East Anglian* N.S. **3**, 1889-90, 23-4. Early 17th c.

Wiveton

See Blakeney

Wymondham

CARTHEW, G.A. 'Extracts from papers in the church chest of Wymondham', *N.A.* **9**, 1884, 121-52 & 240-74. Extracts mainly from 16th c. guild records, giving names.

18. EDUCATIONAL RECORDS

The records of schools can provide the genealogist with a great deal of information. For Norfolk, however, few histories have been published, and even fewer school registers. Those works likely to be of genealogical value are listed here:

Gresham's School

LINNELL, C.L.S., & DOUGLAS, A.B. *Gresham's School history and register, 1555-1954*. Holt: [ ]: [1955]. School at Holt.

Great Yarmouth Grammar School

WHITEHEAD, JOHN BENSON. *The history of Great Yarmouth Grammar School, 1551-1951*. Jarrold & Sons, 1951. Includes various lists of names.

Norwich Grammar School

SAUNDERS, H.W. *A history of Norwich Grammar School*. Norwich: Jarrold & Sons, 1932. Gives many names from the 16th c. onwards.

HARRIES, RICHARD, CATTERMOLE, PAUL, & MACKINTOSH, PETER. *A history of Norwich School*. Norwich: Friends of Norwich School, 1991. Includes section on distinguished pupils, and list of headmasters.

Paston Grammar School

FORDER, C.R. *A history of the Paston Grammar School, North Walsham, Norfolk*. North Walsham: the governors, 1934. Includes many biographical notes on pupils and staff.

For Norfolk students at Cambridge University, see:

VENN, JOHN. 'The matriculation or admission books of Gonville and Caius College, Cambridge: East Anglian admissions from 1560', *East Anglian* N.S. **1-2**, 1885/6-1887/8, passim.

19. EMIGRATION

The descendants of Norfolk men and women are today to be found in many parts of the world. In order to trace them, you need access to records both in England, and in the places where they settled. It is not my purpose here to give a full listing of works on Norfolk emigrants, but merely to provide a select listing of publications which may prove to be of genealogical value. The most substantial works I have seen relate to the colonization of North America:

HARRIS, JOHN RYDEN. *East Anglia and America*. Ipswich: East Anglian Magazine, 1973.

TYACK, N.C.P. 'The humbler puritans of East Anglia and the New England movement: evidence from the court records of the 1630s', *New England historical and genealogical register* **138**, 1984, 79-106.

JEWSON, CHARLES BOARDMAN, ed. *Transcript of three registers of passengers from Great Yarmouth to Holland and New England, 1637-1639*. N.R.S. **25**, 1954. Gives places of origin, ages, and reasons for journey.

COLDHAM, PETER WILSON. *Bonded passengers to America, vol.7: Norfolk Circuit, 1663-1775, comprising the counties of Bedfordshire, Buckinghamshire, Cambridgeshire, Huntingdonshire, Norfolk and Suffolk*. Baltimore: Genealogical Publishing, 1983. Lists convicts transported.

A work of related interest is:

JEWSON, CHARLES B. 'The English Church at Rotterdam and its Norfolk connections', *N.A.* **30**, 1952, 324-37. Gives names of some members from Norwich and Yarmouth in the 1640s.

There is little of substance on the colonial migrations of the nineteenth century. See, however:

HARPER, J.W. 'Norfolk passengers on the *Trade Wind*, 1857', *N.Anc.* **44**(1), 1985, 7-9. List of emigrants to Hobart, Tasmania.

WILLIAMS, J. ROBERT. 'Norfolk emigrants to South Africa, 1820', *N.Anc.* **3**(2), 1983, 24. Brief list, with ages.

FAMILY NAME INDEX

PLACE NAME INDEX